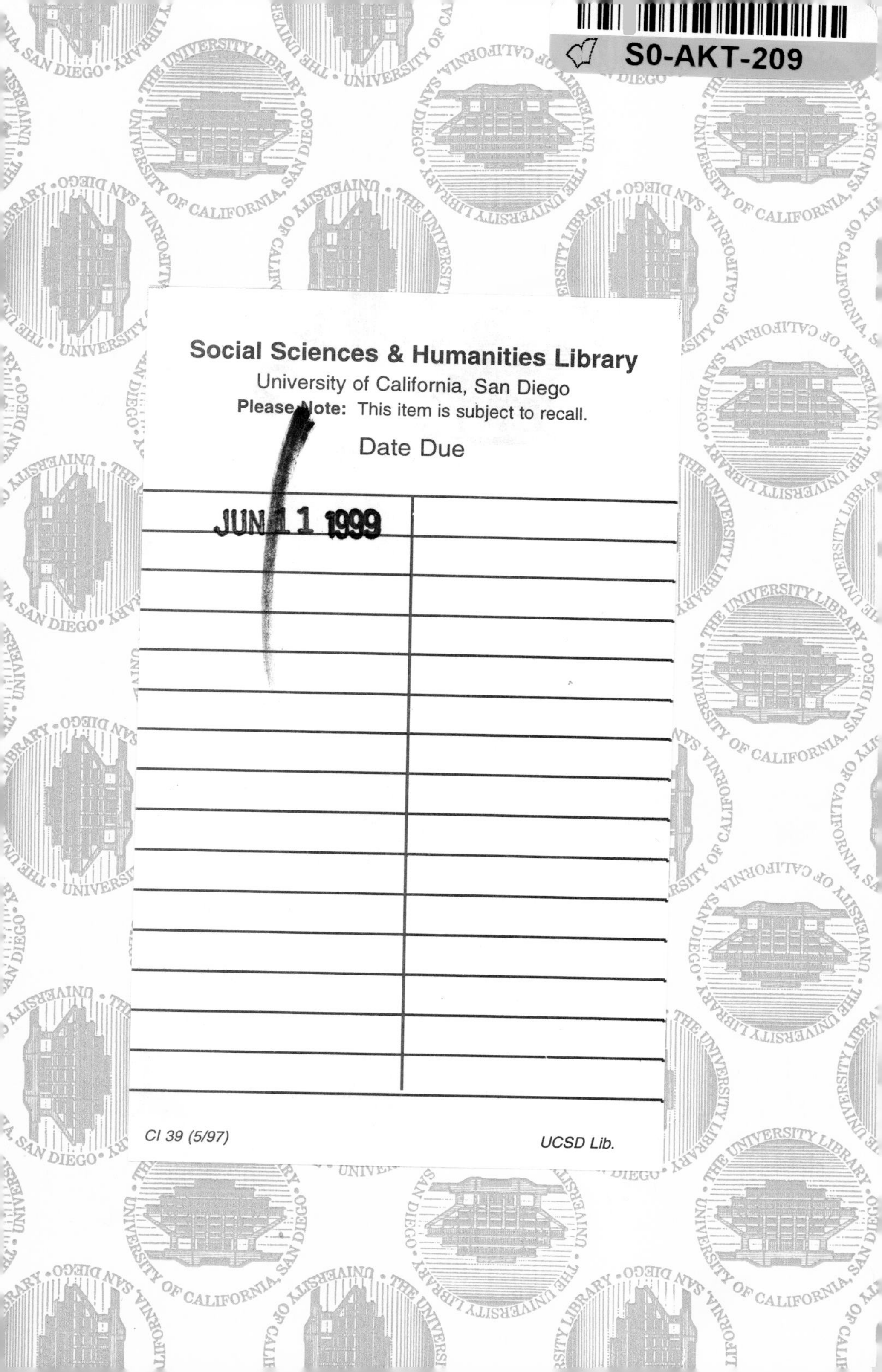

An Anthology of Modern Yiddish Poetry

OTHER BOOKS BY RUTH WHITMAN

POETRY

Hatshepsut, Speak to Me
Laughing Gas: Poems New and Selected 1963–1990
The Testing of Hanna Senesh
Permanent Address: New Poems 1973–1980
Tamsen Donner: A Woman's Journey
The Passion of Lizzie Borden: New and Selected Poems
The Marriage Wig and Other Poems
Blood & Milk Poems

TRANSLATIONS

The Fiddle Rose: Poems 1970–1972 by Abraham Sutzkever
The Selected Poems of Jacob Glatstein
An Anthology of Modern Yiddish Poetry

ESSAYS

Becoming a Poet: Source, Process, and Practice

AN ANTHOLOGY OF MODERN YIDDISH POETRY

BILINGUAL EDITION

THIRD EDITION, REVISED AND ENLARGED

SELECTED AND TRANSLATED BY

RUTH WHITMAN

JACOB GLATSTEIN

RACHEL KORN

ABRAHAM SUTZKEVER

ANNA MARGOLIN

WAYNE STATE UNIVERSITY PRESS   DETROIT

First edition published by October House, 1966
Second edition published by the Education Department of the
Workmen's Circle, 1979
Third edition published by Wayne State University Press, 1995
Detroit, Michigan 48201.

Manufactured in the United States of America.
99 98 97 96 95 5 4 3 2 1

Library of Congress Cataloging-in-Publication Data

An anthology of modern Yiddish poetry : bilingual edition /
selected and translated by Ruth Whitman. — 3rd ed., rev. and enl.
p. cm.
ISBN 0-8143-2533-5 (pbk. : alk. paper)
1. Yiddish poetry—Translations into English.
2. Yiddish poetry. I. Whitman, Ruth, 1922–
PJ5191.E3A56 1995
839'.091308—dc20 94-33004

Designer: Joanne Kinney
Cover art: Drawings of Jacob Glatstein, Rachel Korn,
Abraham Sutzkever, and Anna Margolin
by Morton Sacks.

Grateful acknowledgment is made to the Morris and Emma Schaver
Publication Fund for Jewish Studies for financial assistance in the
publication of this volume.

In memory of my grandfather
JACOB BASSEIN
who came to New York from Borisov, Russia in 1888
who was friend to many Yiddish poets and actors
and who sang me my first Yiddish lullaby

CONTENTS

PREFACE TO THE THIRD EDITION

Since the first publication of this *Anthology* in 1966—the only bilingual anthology then in print—it has enjoyed a continuing and increasing readership. The publication of the second edition by the Workmen's Circle Education Department in 1979 heralded a new proliferation of translations of modern Yiddish poetry, including books of individual poets, as well as anthologies, bilingual and otherwise. All of these have helped to bring more of the rich legacy of twentieth-century Yiddish poetry to the public.

The twenty-eight years since 1966 have seen a great flowering of interest in Yiddish studies on college campuses, schools, and communities across the United States, as well as in Canada and Israel, and in places as remote as Australia and Japan.

The present revised third edition aims to bring the *Anthology* up to date by certain additions and omissions. To further flesh out the role played by women in the original *Anthology*, I have added poems by Celia Dropkin, Rachel Korn, Anna Margolin and Kadya Molodowsky. In the future I hope to devote an anthology entirely to the large group of excellent women poets who have written in Yiddish.

I have been obliged to omit the fine poems by Chaim Grade, for reasons of copyright, but I have added poems by Jacob Glatstein and Abraham Sutzkever, the two giants of Yiddish literature, in an attempt to further round out their selections. I am well aware that no anthology is ever complete, or will satisfy every taste.

My primary objective, from the beginning, was to keep this anthology small and selective, for ease in reading by both new students and lifelong lovers of Yiddish poetry. My aim, as always, has been to choose excellent works that can be transformed into felicitous English poems. I hope, with these further revisions and additions, I have remained true to my vision.

RUTH WHITMAN

ACKNOWLEDGMENTS

Some of these poems first appeared in *The Antioch Review, Bridges, The Call, Delos, Fire Exit, The Graham House Review, Jewish Heritage, The Literary Review, The Massachusetts Review, Midstream, Modern Poetry in Translation, Present Tense, Radix,* and *Tikkun*.

Jacob Glatstein's "Good Night, World," "My Brother Refugee," and "The Joy of the Yiddish Word" were first published in *The Selected Poems of Jacob Glatstein*, translated from the Yiddish and with an introduction by Ruth Whitman (October House, 1972).

Abraham Sutzkever's "The Fiddle Rose," "Fingertips," "My Sister Ethel" and "Prayer for a Sick Friend" were published in *The Fiddle Rose: Poems 1970–1972 by Abraham Sutzkever*, selected and translated by Ruth Whitman, with drawings by Marc Chagall (Wayne State University Press, 1990). "Prayer for a Sick Friend" first appeared in *The New Yorker*.

I owe debts of gratitude to many people: to the MacDowell Colony for several periods of residency during which I worked on this book; to Isaac Bashevis Singer, who gave me the original idea for the book and helped me cut my teeth on his own Yiddish stories; to Michael Astour and Rachel Erlich for their linguistic and critical assistance; and above all, to Robert Szulkin of Brandeis University, my first Yiddish teacher, himself a former student of Abraham Sutzkever in Vilna, who has given me his generous support from the first edition to the present.

A NOTE TO THE SECOND EDITION

I still think that Ruth Whitman's *Anthology of Modern Yiddish Poetry* is a wonderful textbook for those who want to study the Yiddish language and to enjoy what is good in Yiddish poetry.

She has managed to make the translations highly faithful to the Yiddish and at the same time beautiful in English. The choice of poets is excellent.

Of course no anthology can exhaust what Yiddish poets have been creating during hundreds of years. Some new talents have appeared and I expect that a second part of this anthology might come out in the future. But what is given in the first part will surely whet the appetite of all those who love poetry and are interested in Yiddish creativity.

I recommend this book to all schools and all students who are interested in Yiddish poetry and Yiddish literature.

ISAAC BASHEVIS SINGER

TRANSLATOR'S NOTE

Yiddish is a relaxed language, extravagantly hospitable to Hebrew, Polish, Russian, German, and French, lush with a vocabulary full of love terms, diminutives, compounds, and neologisms. To translate this language faithfully into cool rational Anglo-Saxon is extremely challenging. Also, since Yiddish inflections lend themselves far more readily to rhyme than English word endings, I have taken many liberties in the poems that rhyme, sometimes using half-rhymes, internal rhymes, and even alliteration as a substitute, and sometimes omitting the rhyme altogether. I have tried almost always to keep close to the meter of the original, or to give a reasonable approximation of it.

There is little danger of giving away trade secrets about the technique of translation. After I learn the original text as completely as I can—metrically, verbally, and emotionally—there comes a time when I must take the leap into writing an English poem in its own right. But this means that if I abandon a diminutive or transpose a word order; if I use an English idiom which the original only implies, I am doing it conscientiously.

Sometimes the real poem comes full-blown and perfect in the first draft, close to the original, yet with a soul of its own. But this is a sheer gift, as all excellent poetry is a given miracle.

I owe a word of explanation about the selections. All anthologies are necessarily subjective to a degree. I usually found it impossible to translate a poem successfully unless I liked it very much. Poems which I tried to translate out of a sense of duty toward historical completeness or adequate representation usually failed. Some poets, like A. Glanz-Leyeles, who are very important to the history of modern Yiddish poetry, I simply found incompatible with my own poetic capabilities. The poems which are included in this anthology were chosen primarily because they especially fitted my hand and my taste as a poet.

But I believe, with Franz Rosenzweig, "one's time is better spent in translating ten lines than writing the longest disquisition 'about.'"

INTRODUCTION

The past ninety years have seen the spectacular rise and development of Yiddish poetry which, until the beginning of the twentieth century, had remained virtually arcane for six hundred years. Its development as an art form between the thirteenth and the nineteenth centuries was very slender, but it was eclectic, various, and above all, persistent. It reached its full flowering in the twentieth century because the horizon of the European Jew, having broken through the cultural as well as the physical ghetto, became one with the rest of the world. Immigration, especially to the United States, brought new literary experience to the Yiddish writer; the loosening of restrictive laws and customs released him to the contemporary world.

Early Yiddish poetry was of two general types: religious, that is, translations of the Bible, reworkings of biblical stories, such as the rhymed translation of Judith, sabbath songs and holiday songs, and guides to the moral life, entertainingly written especially for women; and secular poetry, much of it reinterpretations of European models, such as ballads, topical poems, animal fables, and satirical poetry. Yiddish poets took over and retold medieval stories of chivalry from English, German, and Italian literature, simply removing the Christian symbolism.

By the end of the eighteenth century Yiddish poetry was in a period of transition. The old traditional ways of thinking were beginning to lose their hold, and for the first time poetry began to show an originality and consciousness of artistic form. The Badchan singers—the merrymakers at Jewish weddings who improvised oral lyrics—produced Eliakum Zunser, who wrote his lyrics, conscious of them as literature, lyrics which now survive as traditional folksongs.

By the end of the nineteenth century the modernization of Jewish life made possible the total Europeanization of its writing. And once Yiddish poetry began to blossom, it did so with the suddenness and illusory expository quality of time-lapse photography. Yet this very rapidity of development sometimes had an adverse effect on individual movements. No sooner did one school or group rise than another sprang up as a reaction to the first. The full development which might have taken place in a special group of poets was thus often abruptly halted.

Yiddish poetry in the last decade of the nineteenth century and the beginning of the twentieth is traditionally associated with Itzik Leyb Peretz, Simon Frug, and especially with Morris Rosenfeld, the poet of the sweatshop. Rosenfeld came to the United States at the end of the last century and began his career by contributing protest poetry to the American Yiddish press, which was then being newly established in New York. Although he was primarily a folk poet, he was a pioneer lyricist who treated Yiddish not as a bizarre phenomenon or a haphazard jargon, but as a genuine medium for poetic communication.

More important, both as poet and innovator, was Rosenfeld's contemporary, Yehoash (Solomon Bloomgarten). Yehoash too came to the United States at the end of the last century, and carried Yiddish poetry a step further. For him poetry was no longer the handmaiden of politics, the voice of social protest, but highly personal, full of meditations on love, nature, and metaphysics. His technical repertory was more complex than Rosenfeld's, but neither of them had come fully into the twentieth-century experience; both were still largely characterized by the sentimentality of the Victorian legacy.

Yehoash is especially famous for his translation of the Old Testament into Yiddish and his work in the field of lexicography. He was the immediate predecessor of the first important group of Yiddish poets in America, Di Yunge (The Young Ones). It is with the members of this group that modern Yiddish poetry and the selections in this anthology begin.

Di Yunge was the American version of a poetic movement which appeared in Yiddish literature simultaneously in Russia, Poland, and the United States. Yiddish writers in all three countries were influenced by Heinrich Heine, by impressionism in Europe, especially Germany, and by the Russian symbolists. This impressionism had a distinct tinge of romanticism, in which the emphasis was upon individuality, subjectivity, and a free and indirect method of expression.

In Russia, Leyb Naydus was one of the Yiddish exponents of impressionism. Influenced greatly by European poetry, which he translated, he especially wanted to free himself from the rigidity of traditionalism.

In America, members of Di Yunge—H. Leivick, Zisha Landau, Moyshe Leyb Halpern, and others—were most active in the years 1907 to 1925. Young in years, wildly energetic, fearlessly imaginative, these poets believed politics, propaganda, sentimentality, moralizing, and chauvinism had no place in their poetry. Like the imagists, they were intensely interested in form. They wrote with equal intensity, and perhaps perversity, about the most trivial as well as the most exalted subjects.

All these poets were immigrants and reflected the chaos and complexity of their new life. Zisha Landau is the outstanding exponent of art for art's sake; his poetry was strongly idiosyncratic and sensuous. There were those to whom subject matter was of greater importance, like H. Leivick and M. L. Halpern. Of these, M. L. Halpern was undoubtedly the most original of the group, both as poet and person. He is brash, daring, at one moment filled with enthusiasm, at the next reflecting bitterly and grotesquely on death. Even his diction oscillates between beautifully refined lines and jarring, almost brutal passages.

For all their apparent coarseness, superficiality and extremism, Di Yunge did Yiddish poetry a great service. Their experimentation in technique, their spontaneity, even their Bohemian lives served to fulfil a need in Yiddish literature. But Di Yunge were bound to burn themselves out. Their breakneck speed in both life and poetry made them bypass the slower process of maturity. They had to give way to the inevitable reaction of a new group, the Insichists (Introspectivists).

The First World War and the Russian Revolution had changed the outlook of Yiddish literature. This generation of writers had been shocked out of their complacency and needed to establish their identity in new terms. The Insichists, led by A. Glanz-Leyeles, N. Minkoff, and Jacob Glatstein, profiting from the experience of Di Yunge, were more serious, more intellectual, and more eager to include a view of the outer world. It must be noted, however, that as a school neither Di Yunge nor the Insichists adhered rigidly to any strict set of poetic principles or world view.

What guided them was the general principle of inner freedom: the Insichists wanted to express in their poetry the refraction of the outer world as seen through the prism of the individual self (*sich*) or ego. They used new methods and forms, especially free verse. In their magazine and anthology, both called *In Sich*, they published, among many others, the poetry of Anna Margolin, a fiery bohemian, who wrote a passionate, disciplined poetry.

Both of these major American movements in Yiddish poetry before the Second World War produced poets of world stature. Although H. Leivick and Jacob Glatstein, associated with Di Yunge and with the Insichists respectively, are exponents of these schools, they are primarily significant as great poets.

Leivick, a political prisoner in Siberia, escaped to the United States in 1913 and was immediately claimed by Di Yunge as one of their own. He was a most prolific writer, following the theme of the Messiah through verse play after verse play. The Nazi extermination of the Jews increased the personal guilt he had always felt about his suffering fellow men in other countries, and this too became a major theme in both his plays and lyric poetry. A master of short forms, he is one of the few poets anywhere who combines in one person both lyric and dramatic genius.

Glatstein's poetic standpoint and resources are perhaps the widest of any poet represented in this anthology. He is also in many ways the most difficult poet. He is a supremely original manipulator of the Yiddish language. He makes up words, combines words, deals in stunning imagery and in bold and sometimes angry conceptions. A sensitive and articulate critic and novelist, he resembles T. S. Eliot in his intensity, difficulty, and lyricism. Also, although he began as a member of the Insichists, he has, since the Second World War, been moved to re-examine his role as individual in the world. In consequence, he has combined a cauterizing classicism and traditionalism with his original audacious approach.

In Poland, a major center of Yiddish culture and literature before the Second World War, a parallel post-impressionist movement took place. Influenced by German expressionism and Russian cubo-futurism, a group was formed who called themselves Di Khaliastre (The Gang). Doting on the grotesque and decadent, these poets also stressed individuality and audacity. They included Melech Ravitch, who, now in the New World, still carried on an incessant familiar dialogue with God, haranguing and ranting in swashbuckling lines and language. Other writers who began their careers in Poland were Aaron Zeitlin, who, in addition to using post-impressionist techniques and ideas, was deeply imbued with classical tradition; and Moyshe Kulbak, who wrote with a poetic vigor and dynamism, a bravado not unlike that of early Mayakovsky, and later identified himself with Soviet Yiddish literature until he disappeared mysteriously in 1937.

Despite the anti-Semitism of the Polish government and the desperate conditions after the First World War, three of these poets—Aaron Zeitlin, Melech Ravitch, and Kadya Molodowsky, a novelist and short story writer as well as a children's poet—survived to come to the United States and Canada, and continued to write there.

By the end of the 1920's, both in Europe and the United States, Yiddish poetry no longer felt threatened, it no longer had to argue and polemicize. It was. Heine, German impressionism, Rilke, Baudelaire, the French and Russian symbolists, Whitman, the American imagists, free forms, expressionism, surrealism, the use of conversational vocabulary and rhythms—all these were grist to its mill.

Although by the 1930's the literary schools had ceased to play as dominant a role as they had earlier, there were various groups and subgroups on both sides of the Atlantic, especially on the regional level. Just before the Second World War, one such group, the Young Vilna poets, produced two outstanding men, Chaim Grade, a short story writer and novelist who came to live in New York, and Abraham Sutzkever.

Sutzkever is extremely gifted, as is evident from his experimental pantheistic beginnings to his latest poems in *Di Goldene Keyt* (The Golden Chain), a Yiddish journal which he publishes and edits in Israel. He is not only a master manipulator of language, somewhat in the style of Glatstein, but has a pervasive sensual lyricism. His vision and imagery is often Chagall-like in its playful eroticism and use of surrealist techniques. His thematic geography runs from the steppes of Siberia through the Vilna Ghetto to the woods of Lithuania to Israel and the Sinai desert, and even includes the exotica of Africa.

The expressionists brought Yiddish poetry to a point of stabilization. The wild rebellion of the early years became tempered with a new classicism, an independent return to traditionalism. The Hitler era and the Second World War greatly strengthened this tendency. Jewish writers felt impelled to re-examine their heritage, to reaffirm their lines of continuity with the past, and to rediscover and honor their literary traditions.

In Poland one of the most outstanding of these neoclassical poets was Rachel Korn (who finally came to live in Canada), who writes with a deceptive simplicity, a pure lyricism.

In Romania the direction toward traditionalism followed a similar course. Mingling impressionistic techniques with folk and classical forms, Itzik Manger not only experimented with Old Yiddish and wrote eccentric anti-poetry, but also was capable of writing short ballads on themes from the Old Testament with tenderness, humor, and a sense of the outlandish.

Russia has always been an important center for Yiddish poetry, both before the purges (Peretz Markish, Leyb Kvitko, and Itzik Fefer were among the important poets liquidated by Stalin) and after. In 1965 an anthology was published containing the work of fifty Russian Yiddish poets.

A history of these many Yiddish poets, both living and dead, must still be written. This account merely provides a framework for the selections represented in this anthology and gives only a hint of the rich poetry which has scarcely been glimpsed by English and American critics and readers.

Certainly the moment of ripening of Yiddish poetry possesses a terrible historical irony. For just when Yiddish poetry had entered the mainstream of modern European and American literature, overcoming the handicaps of history through its sheer will and dynamism, the Nazi genocide and Soviet purges destroyed many of the writers and readers of Yiddish. But there are poets and novelists writing in Yiddish today in the United States, in Israel, Canada, South America, Mexico, France and the USSR. Yiddish poetry in the twentieth century may well be the most enduring artistic expression of its people's creative vitality.

RUTH WHITMAN
ROBERT SZULKIN

An Anthology of Modern Yiddish Poetry

די צירקוס־דאַמע

איך בין אַ צירקוס־דאַמע
און טאַנץ צווישן קינזשאַלן,
וואָס זײַנען אויפֿגעשטעלט אויף דער אַרענע
מיט די שפּיצן אַרויף.
מײַן בייגזאַם לײַכטער גוף
מײַדט אויס דעם טויט פֿון פֿאַלן,
באַרירנדיק קוים, קוים דעם שאַרף פֿון די קינזשאַלן.

מיט אַ פֿאַרכאַפּטן אָטעם קוקט מען אויף מײַן טאַנצן,
און עמעץ בעט דאָרט פֿאַר מיר גאָט.
פֿאַר מײַנע אויגן גלאַנצן
די שפּיצן אין אַ פֿײַערדיקן ראָד, —
און קיינער ווייס ניט, ווי מיר ווילט זיך פֿאַלן.

מיד בין איך פֿון טאַנצן צווישן אײַך,
קאַלטע שטאָלענע קינזשאַלן.
איך וויל מײַן בלוט זאָל אײַך דערהיצן,
אויף אײַערע אָנטבלויזטע שפּיצן
וויל איך פֿאַלן.

CELIA DROPKIN

The Circus Lady

I'm a circus lady,
I dance between the knives
standing in the ring,
tips pointing up.
My lightly bending body
avoids death from falling
by brushing lightly, lightly against the blades.

Breathless, they watch me dance
and someone prays for me.
Before my eyes the points
flash in a fiery wheel,—
and no one knows how I want to fall.

I'm tired of dancing between
you, cold steel knives.
I want my blood to scald you,
I want to fall
on your naked tips.

מײַנע הענט

מײַנע הענט,
צוויי שטיקלעך פֿון מײַן לײַב,
וואָס איך שעם מיך ניט צו צײַגן,
מיט פֿינגער, ווי די צווײַגן
פֿון אַ קאָראַלן־בוים.
מיט פֿינגער, ווי צוויי נעסטן
ווײַסע שלאַנגען.
אָדער . . . ווי געדאַנקען
פֿון אַן עראָטאָמאַן.

My Hands

My hands,
two pieces of my body
that I'm not ashamed to show,
with fingers like the branches
of a coral tree,
with fingers like two nests
of white snakes.
Or—like the thoughts
of a lecherous man.

1948

אָדם

אַ צעלאָזענעם,
אַן אויסגעצערטלטן פֿון פֿילע פֿרויענהענט,
האָב איך דיר אויף מײַן וועג געטראָפֿן,
יונגער אָדם.
און איידער איך האָב צוגעלייגט צו דיר מײַנע ליפּן,
האָסטו מיך געבעטן
מיט אַ פּנים, בלאַסער און צאַרטער
פֿון דער צאַרטסטער ליליע:
– ניט בײַס מיך, ניט בײַס מיך.
איך האָב דערזען, אַז דײַן לײַב
איז אין גאַנצן באַדעקט מיט צייכנס פֿון ציינער,
אַ פֿאַרציטערטע האָב איך זיך אין דיר אײַנגעביסן.
דו האָסט פֿונאַנדערגעבלאָזן איבער מיר
דײַנע דינע נאָזלעכער,
און האָסט זיך צוגערוקט צו מיר,
ווי אַ הייסער האָריזאָנט צום פֿעלד.

Adam

You, spoiled,
fondled by the hands of many women,
I came upon you by chance,
young Adam.
And before I could lay my mouth on yours,
you begged me
with the pale tender face
of the tenderest lily:
—Don't bite me, don't bite me.
I saw that your body
was completely covered with teethmarks.
Trembling, I bit into you.
You flared your thin nostrils
over me
and edged close to me
like a burning horizon against a field.

אַ מורא איז געוואַקסן אין מײַן האַרץ

אַ מורא איז געוואַקסן אין מײַן האַרץ:
איך האָב געשפּירט דעם פֿוילן ריח
פֿון מײַן קבֿר אַרום זיך.
און די נײַע זײַדענע גאַרדינען אויפֿן טיר
האָבן שטיל מײַן נאָענטן טויט באַדויערט:
„מיר וועלן בלײַבן באַלד אָן דיר,
מיר וועלן בלײַבן באַלד אָן דיר".
ווי נאַריש וואָס איך האָב זיך איצטער, פֿאַרן טויט
מיט זאַכן זײַדענע פֿאַרגרייט!
און מאָדנע טרויעריק האָב איך געטראַכט,
אַז אין מײַן ערדישן אַלקאָוו
וועל איך ניט האָבן קיין זײַדענע גאַרדינען,
אַפֿילו ניט קיין אונטערוועש פֿון זײַד. —
נאָר פּלוצלינג האָב איך צו זיך געזאָגט:
דײַנע גלידער זײַנען, ווי פֿון העלפֿאַנטביין געשניצט.
ווי אַ רויך מײַן שרעק צעגייט:
איך בין פֿון טויט באַשיצט!

A Terror Was Rising in My Heart

A terror was rising in my heart:
I could smell the odor of decay
around my grave.
And the new silk draperies on the door
were silently lamenting my coming death:
"We'll soon be without you,
we'll soon be without you."
How foolish I was to prepare
silken things before my death!
How odd and sad to think
that in my earthen alcove
I would have no silken draperies,
not even underwear of silk.
But just now I suddenly said to myself:
Your arms and legs look like elephant bone.
And my terror disappeared like smoke:
Death will surely reject me!

אָ גוטע נאַכט, וועלט

אָ גוטע נאַכט, ברייטע וועלט,
גרויסע, שטינקענדיקע וועלט.
נישט דו, נאָר איך פֿאַרהאַק דעם טויער.
מיט דעם לאַנגן כאַלאַט,
מיט דער פֿײַערדיקער, געלער לאַט,
מיט דעם שטאָלצן טראָט,
אויף מײַן אייגענעם געבאָט —
גיי איך צוריק אין געטאָ.
וויש אָפ, צעטרעט אַלע געשמדטע שפורן.
כ'וואַלגער זיך אין דײַן מיסט,
לויב, לויב, לויב,
צעהויקערט ייִדיש לעבן.
חרם, וועלט, אויף דײַנע טריפֿהנע קולטורן.
כאָטש אַלץ איז פֿאַרוויסט,
שטויב איך זיך אין דײַן שטויב,
טרויעריק ייִדיש לעבן.

חזירישער דאַטש, פֿײַנטלעכער ליאַד,
עמלק גנבֿ, לאַנד פֿון זויפֿן און פֿרעסן.
שלאַברע דעמאָקראַטיע, מיט דײַנע קאַלטע
סימפאַטיע־קאָמפרעסן.
אָ גוטע נאַכט, עלעקטריש צעחוצפהטע וועלט.
צוריק צו מײַן קעראָסין, חלבֿנעם שאָטן,
אייביקן אָקטאָבער, דריבנע שטערן,
צו מײַנע קרומע גאַסן, הויקערדיקן לאַמטערן,
מײַנע שמות, מײַן סוואַרבע,
מײַנע גמרות, צו די האַרבע
סוגיות, צום ליכטיקן עבֿרי־טײַטש,
צום דין, צום טיפֿן מיין, צום חובֿ, צום גערעכט,
וועלט, איך שפאַן מיט פֿרייד צום שטילן געטאָ־לעכט.

JACOB GLATSTEIN

GOOD NIGHT, WORLD

Good night, wide world,
big stinking world.
Not you but I slam shut the gate.
With a long gabardine,
with a fiery yellow patch,
with a proud stride,
because I want to,
I'm going back to the ghetto.
Wipe away, stamp out every vestige of conversion.
I roll around in your garbage—
praise, praise, praise—
hunchbacked Jewish life.
Damn your dirty culture, world.
I wallow in your dust
even though it's forsaken,
sad Jewish life.

German pig, cutthroat Pole,
Rumania, thief, land of drunkards and gluttons.
Weak-kneed democracy, with your cold
sympathy-compresses.
Good night, electrified arrogant world.
Back to my kerosene, candle shadows,
eternal October, tiny stars,
to my crooked streets, humped lanterns,
my sacred pages, my Bible,
my Gemorra, to my backbreaking
studies, to the bright Yiddish prayerbook,
to law, profundity, duty, justice,—
world, I walk gladly towards quiet ghetto light.

אָ גוטע נאַכט, כ׳גיב דיר, וועלט, צו שטײַער
אַלע מײַנע באַפֿרײַער.
נעם צו די יעזוס־מאַרקסעס, ווערג זיך מיט זייער מוט.
קראַפּיר איבער אַ טראָפּן פֿון אונדזער געטויפֿט בלוט.
און איך האָב האָפֿן אַז כאָטש ער זאַמט זיך,
גייט אויף טאָג־אײַן טאָג־אויס מײַן וואַרטן.
ס׳וועלן נאָך רוישן גרינע בלעטער
אויף אונדזער בוים דעם פֿאַרקוואַרטן.
איך דאַרף קיין טרייסט נישט.
איך גיי צוריק צו דלד אַמות,
פֿון וואַנגערס געצמוזיק, צו ניגון, ברומען.
כ׳קוש דיך, פֿאַרקאָלטנט ייִדיש לעבן.
ס׳ויינט אין מיר די פֿרייד פֿון קומען.

Good night. I'll make you, world, a gift of
all my liberators.
Take back your Jesus-Marxes, choke on their courage.
Croak over a drop of our christianized blood.
For I have hope, even if He is delaying,
day by day my expectation rises.
Green leaves will yet rustle
on our sapless tree.
I don't need any consolation.
I'm going back to my very beginnings,
from Wagner's pagan music to melody, to humming.
I kiss you, disheveled Jewish life,
I cry with the joy of coming back.

August 1938

מײַן וואָגל־ברודער

כ'האָב ליב מײַן טרויעריקן גאָט,
מײַן וואָגל־ברודער.
כ'האָב ליב זיך צוצוזעצן מיט אים אויף אַ שטיין
און אויסשטומען פֿון זיך אַלע רייד.
ווײַל אַז מיר זיצן אַזוי ביידע געפּלעפּט,
ווערן אונדזערע מחשבֿות באַהעפֿט –
אין שווײַגן.

*　*　*　*　*

ס'צינדט זיך אַ שטערן, אַ פֿײַערדיקן אות.
זײַנע גלידער בענקען נאָך שלאָף,
די נאַכט ליגט אונדז צופֿוסנס ווי אַ שאָף.

מײַן טײַערער גאָט,
וויפֿל תּפֿילות צו אים האָב איך פֿאַרשווערכט.
וויפֿל מאָל האָב איך אים געלעסטערט,
דורך די נעכט,
און געוואַרעמט די שרעקעוודיקע ביינער
בײַם פֿײַערטאָפּ פֿון וויסן.
און דאָ זיצט ער, מײַן חבֿר, נעמט מיך אַרום,
און טיילט מיט מיר דעם לעצטן ביסן.

דער גאָט פֿון מײַן אומגלויבן איז פּרעכטיק,
ווי ליב איז מיר מײַן פֿאַרשלאָפֿטער גאָט,
איצט ווען ער איז מענטשלעך און אומגערעכטיק.
ווי דערהויבן איז דער שטאָלצער יורד,
ווען ס'מינדסטע קינד איז מורד
אין זײַן געבאָט.

My Brother Refugee

I love my sad God,
my brother refugee.
I love to sit down on a stone with him
and tell him everything wordlessly
because when we sit like this, both perplexed,
our thoughts flow together
in silence.

* * * * *

A star lights up, a fiery letter.
His body longs for sleep.
The night leans like a sheep against our feet.

My poor God,
how many prayers I've profaned,
how many nights I've
blasphemed him
and warmed my frightened bones
at the furnace of the intellect.
And here he sits, my friend, his arm around me,
sharing his last crumb.

The God of my unbelief is magnificent,
how I love my unhappy God
now that he's human and unjust.
How exalted is this proud pauper
now that the merest child rebels
against his word.

* * * * *

דו רעדסט פֿון זיך,
שווײַגט צו מיר מײַן וואָגל־ברודער,
און איך טראַכט פֿון אונדז אַלעמען,
אַזוי צו זאָגן:

וויפֿל חורבן דאַרף אַ פֿאָלק פֿאַרטראָגן,
אַז ס׳זאָל אין אויפֿבוי אַלץ נאָך גלייבן.

איצט אַז ס׳וואָלגערט זיך אין שטויבן,
איז דאָס פֿאָלק געטלעכער פֿון מיר.
ס׳וועלן נאָך פֿעלקער קומען זיך בוקן
צו זײַן ווייטיק.

אָבער גאָט, מײַן ברודער,
צו וואָס האָסטו אַזוי דערהויבן מײַן פֿאָלק
און צעשטערנט זײַן אומגליק
איבערן גאַנצן הימל?

ווייטיק, בלוט, געלעכערטע הענט,
רחמנות פֿון אויסגערונענע אָדערן —
אַ קינדערשער משל מיט נאַרישע רייד.
איך האָב עס געכּפּלט אויף זעקס מיליאָן,
איך האָב דעם משל געגעבן באַשייד.
מײַן פֿאָלק, מײַן זון, מײַן טרוים.
ווערט אייביק בליִען געקרייציקט אויף אַ ליכטיקן בוים.

מײַן גאָט שלאָפֿט און איך וואַך איבער אים.
מײַן מידער ברודער חלומט דעם חלום פֿון מײַן פֿאָלק.
ער ווערט קליין ווי אַ קינד,
און איך וויג אים אײַן אין חלום פֿון מײַן פֿאָלק.
שלאָף, מײַן גאָט, מײַן וואָגל־ברודער,
שלאָף אַרײַן אין חלום פֿון מײַן פֿאָלק.

* * * * *

You're talking to me silently
about yourself, brother refugee,
but I am thinking about all of us,
so to speak:

How much destruction can a people suffer
and still believe in rebuilding?

Now that they're wallowing in dust
my people are godlier than I am.
Nations will yet bow
to their anguish.

But God, my brother,
why have you exalted my people like this,
constellating their misfortune
across the whole sky?

Suffering, blood, pierced hands,
the pity of bloodless veins—
a childish fable with foolish words.
I've multiplied that by six million,
I've given that fable a moral.
My people, my son, my dream will bloom
crucified forever on a shining tree.

My God sleeps while I keep watch,
my tired brother dreams the dream of my people.
He's small as a child
and I rock him into the dream.
Sleep, my God, my brother refugee,
sleep, and vanish into our dream.

מאָצאַרט

ס׳האָט זיך מיר געחלומט,
גויים האָבן מאָצאַרטן געקרייציקט
און אים באַגראָבן אין אַן אייזל־קבֿר.
נאָר ייִדן האָבן אים געמאַכט פֿאַר גאָטס מענטש
און זײַן געדעכעניש געבענטשט.

זײַן אַפּאָסטאָל בין איך איבער דער וועלט געלאָפֿן
און באַקערט יעדער איינעם וואָס כ׳האָב געטראָפֿן.
אומעטום וווּ כ׳האָב געכאַפּט אַ קריסט,
האָב איך אים געשמדט אויף אַ מאָצאַרטיסט.

ווי וווּנדערלעך איז פֿון געטלעכן מענטש
זײַן מוזיקאַלישער טעסטאַמענט,
ווי דורכגענאָגלט מיט געזאַנג
זײַנען זײַנע ליכטיקע הענט.
אין זײַן גרעסטער נויט,
האָבן בײַם געקרייציקטן זינגער
געלאַכט אַלע פֿינגער.
אין זײַן ווייִנענדיקסטן טרויער,
האָט ער נאָך מער ווי זיך אַליין
ליב געהאַט דעם שכנס אויער.

ווי אָרעם און ווי קאַרג,
אַנטקעגן מאָצאַרטס פֿאַרבלײַב,
איז די דרשה אויפֿן באַרג.

Mozart

I dreamed that
the gentiles crucified Mozart
and buried him in a pauper's grave.
But the Jews made him a man of God
and blessed his memory.

I, his apostle, ran all over the world,
converting everyone I met,
and wherever I caught a Christian
I made him a Mozartian.

How wonderful is the musical testament
of this divine man!
How nailed through with song
his shining hands!
In his greatest need
all the fingers of this crucified
singer were laughing.
And in his most crying grief
he loved his neighbor's ear
more than himself.

How poor and stingy—
compared with Mozart's legacy—
is the Sermon on the Mount.

נאַכטלידער

פֿרעמדע אויגן זעען נישט,
ווי אין מײַן קלײנעם חדר עפֿן איך אַ טיר,
און צווישן קבֿרים הייבט זיך אָן מײַן נאַכטיקער שפּאַציר.
(וויפֿל ערד, מישטיינס געזאָגט, דאַרפֿן רויכן?)
פֿאַראַן דאַרטן טאָלן און הויכן
און באַהאַלטענע, פֿאַרדרייטע שטעגן,
וואָס קלעקן אויף אַ גאַנצן נאַכטיקן גאַנג.
אין דער פֿינצטער לויכטן מיר אַנטקעגן
פּה־נטמנס,
מיט אַ יעמערלעך געזאַנג.
ס׳בליִען קבֿרים פֿון דער גאַנצער
פֿאַרטיליקטער ייִדישער וועלט,
אין די דלד אָמות פֿון מײַן געצעלט,
און איך בעט:
זײַט מיר אַ טאַטע, אַ מאַמע,
אַ שוועסטער, אַ ברודער,
קינדער אייגענע, לײַבלעכע קרובֿים,
ווערט וואָר ווי צער,
פֿון אייגן בלוט און פֿלייש,
זײַט צו מיר געשטאָרבן,
לאָזט מיך משׂיג זײַן און אָנען
דעם חורבן פֿון מיליאָנען.

פֿאַר טאָג פֿאַרמאַך איך די טיר,
צום בית־הקבֿרות פֿון מײַן פֿאָלק.
איך זיץ בײַם טיש און פֿאַרדרימל זיך
מיטן ברומען פֿון אַ ניגון.
דער שׂונא האָט אויף זיי נישט געהאַט קיין שליטה.
טאַטעס, מאַמעס, קינדער פֿון די וויגן,
האָבן אַרומגערינגלט דעם טויט און אים אײַנגענומען,

Nightsongs

Strangers' eyes don't see
how in my small room I open a door
and begin my nightly stroll among the graves.
(How much earth—if you can call it earth—
 does it take to bury smoke?)
There are valleys and hills
and hidden twisted paths,
enough to last a whole night's journey.
In the dark I see shining towards me
faces of epitaphs
wailing their song.
Graves of the whole
vanished Jewish world
blossom in my one-man tent.
And I pray:
Be a father, a mother to me,
a sister, a brother,
my own children, body–kin,
real as pain,
from my own blood and skin,
be my own dead,
let me grasp and take in
these destroyed millions.

At dawn I shut the door
to my people's house of death.
I sit at the table and doze off,
humming a tune.
The enemy had no dominion over them.
Fathers, mothers, children from their cradles
ringed around death and overcame him.

אַלע קליינע קינדער זײַנען פֿאַרוווּנדערט
געלאָפֿן דעם טויט־שרעק אַקעגן,
אָן געוויינען, ווי פֿאַרוויגטע ייִדישע מעשׂהלעך קליינע.
און באַלד האָבן זיי אויפֿגעפֿלאַקערט אין פֿלעמלעך,
ווי קליינע אַדוישעמלעך.

ווער האָט נאָך, ווי איך,
אַזאַ אייגענעם, בײַנאַכטיקן,
טויטן גאָרטן?
וועמען איז נאָך דאָרטן אַזוי באַשערט ווי מיר?
אויף ווענמען וואַרט אַזוי פֿיל טויטע ערד ווי אויף מיר?
ווען איך וועל שטאַרבן,
ווער וועט אַרבן מײַן קליינעם בית־הקבֿרות,
און דאָס ליכטיקע געשאַנק,
פֿון אַ נר־תּמידיק יאָרצײַט־ליכט,
אין אייביקן געצאַנק?

All the children, astonished,
ran to meet the fear of death
without tears, like little Jewish bedtime stories.
And soon they flickered into flames
like small namesakes of God.

Who else, like me, has
his own nighttime
dead garden?
Who is destined for this, as I am?
Who has so much dead earth waiting for him, as for me?
And when I die
who will inherit my small house of death
and that shining gift,
  an eternal deathday light
forever flickering?

כ׳װעל זיך אײַנגלױבערן

כ׳װעל זיך אײַנגלױבערן אין דעם שטױבעלע װוּנדער,
װאָס פֿלעקט דעם אױסזיכט אױף צוריק,
אַזױ װײַט װי דער טונקעלער בליק
קען צוריקחלומען, צוריקזען.
אין דעם אױפֿגעטױכטן,
אױפֿגעלױכטן טונקל,
העלט אױף אַ האַלבער
אָפּגעראַטעװעטער שטערן,
װאָס האָט נישט באַװיזן חרובֿ צו װערן.
אַ שטיק אױפֿגעריסענער פּלאַנעט
װאָס האָט אַ מאָל געהאַט לעבן,
גרינע שפּע, פּאַשעדיקע זעט.
עדות: מײַנע טרערן־פֿאַרלאָפֿענע אױגן,
די װײַטע פֿלאָראַ, די בלוט־באַטרױבטע,
אונטער אַ הימל פֿון אײביקן אונטערגאַנג;
די בלעטער, װאָס װיגן זיך װי גלעקער,
באַטױבטע, אָן קלאַנג,
אױף פֿון־קײנעם־נישט־געזעענע בײמער
אין אַ לײדיקער װעלט.

כ׳װעל זיך אײַנעקשנען,
זיך אײַנפֿלאַנצן
אין אַן אײגענער, אינטימער נאַכט,
װאָס איך האָב אין גאַנצן אױסגעטראַכט
און אַרומגעװוּנדערט פֿון אַלע זײַטן.
כ׳װעל געפֿינען אַן אָרט אין רױם,
װי אַ פֿליג די גרײס,
און מיט גװאַלד אַװעקשטעלן דאָרט,
אױף אַלע צײַטן
אַ װיג, אַ קינד,
אַרײַנזינגען אין דעם אַ קול

I'll Find My Self-Belief

I'll find my self-belief in a dustpuff of wonder
flecking my view back
as far as dim sight
can imagine, can see.
In the bobbing
kindled dark
there rises up
a salvaged half-star
that managed not to be killed.
A chunk of exploded planet
that once had life,
green abundance, grazing luxury.
Witnesses: my tearfilled eyes,
the distant flora, grapestained with blood,
under a sky eternally sinking;
leaves rocking like bells
deafened, soundless,
on unlooked-at trees
in an empty world.

I'll be stubborn,
plant myself
in my own intimate night
which I've entirely invented
and admired from all sides.
I'll find my place in space
as big as a fly,
and compel to stand there
for all time
a cradle, a child,
into whom I'll sing the voice

פֿון אַ דרימלענדיקן טאַטן,
מיט אַ פּנים אין קול,
מיט ליבשאַפֿט אין קול,
מיט פֿאַרהויכטע אויגן,
וואָס שווימען אין קינדס שלעפֿעריקע אויגן
ווי וואַרעמע לבֿנות.
און אויפֿבויען וועל איך אַרום דער וויג אַ ייִדישע שטאָט
מיט אַ שול, מיט א לאַ־ינומדיקן גאָט,
וואָס וואַכט איבער די אָרעמע קראָמען,
איבער ייִדישן פּחד,
איבער דעם בית־עולם,
וואָס איז לעבעדיק אַ גאַנצע נאַכט
מיט פֿאַרדאגהטע מתים.

כ׳וועל זיך אײַנקלאַמערן מיט די לעצטע טעג,
און אויף להכעיס זיי ציילן אין דיר, פֿאַרגליווערטער עבֿר,
וואָס האָסט מיך אויסגעלאַכט,
וואָס האָסט אויסגעטראַכט
מײַן לעבעדיקע, ריידעוודיקע
ייִדישע וועלט.
די אײַנגעשטיליקט,
און אין מײַדאַנעק־וועלדל
מיט עטלעכע שאָס פֿאַרטיליקט.

of a father drowsing,
with a face in the voice,
with love in the voice,
with hazy eyes
that swim in the child's sleepy eyes
like warm moons.
And I'll build around this cradle a Jewish city
with a *shul*, with a God who never sleeps,
who watches over the poor shops,
over Jewish fear,
over the cemetery
that's lively all night
with worried corpses.

And I'll buckle myself up with my last days
and, for spite, count them in you, frozen past
who mocked me,
who invented
my living, garrulous
Jewish world.
You silenced it
and in Maidanek woods
finished it off with a few bullets.

דער פּאָעט לעבט

דער פּאָעט לעבט. די ייִדישע לוויה־פֿייגל שנאַפּן.
דײַן געזאַנג איז אַ שמירה קעגן זייער געקלאַג.
די לוויה־פֿייגל וועלן דיך ניט כאַפּן,
הײַנט אין דײַן לעבעדיקן פֿאַרטאָג.

דער שפּיגל זוניקט דײַן געשטאַלט.
ער באַהאַלט דײַנע יאָרן מיט אַ פֿאַרגלעט.
פֿאַרשניפּסט דעם האַלדז מיט די שענסטע קאָלירן.
האָב נישט קיין מורא. די ייִדישע לוויה־פֿייגל וועלן דיך ניט באַרירן.
זיי ווילן חלילה ניט זאָגן קיין גוט־מאָרגן אַ לעבעדיקן פּאָעט.

זיי שאַרפֿן שוין די שנאָבלען אויף אַ געקלאָג.
זיי פֿײַפֿן זיך שוין אײַן דעם נעקראָלאָג.
ניט צוליב דיר, נאָר כּדי מיט דײַן טויט צו פֿאַרקריצן,
זייער אָנלויף פֿון אַלע זומפּיקע ווינקלען,
פֿון אַלע אונדזערע פֿאַרשימלטע שטינקלען.

זײַ רויִק, לעבעדיקער פּאָעט.
קאָנסט וויינען, לאַכן, זיך רײַסן אין איינזאַמקייט די האָר.
די לוויה־פֿייגל וועלן שנאַפּן,
אָבער זיי וועלן דיר, חלילה, נישט ווינטשן קיין לעבעדיק יאָר.

The Poet Lives

The poet lives. The Jewish coffin-birds snap.
Your song is a charm against their teasing.
The coffin-birds won't grab you
on this your living morning.

The mirror suns your image.
Your years disappear with a wipe.
Necktie your neck with the prettiest colors.
Don't be afraid. The Jewish coffin-birds won't collar you.
They won't even give the time of day to a living poet.

Now they're honing their beaks to tease you,
they're whistling up your obituary,
not for your sake, but hoping your death will engrave
their arrival from all swampy corners,
from all our moldy stinks.

Be calm, living poet.
Cry, laugh, in solitude tear your hair.
The coffin-birds will peck at you
but they'll never, God forbid, wish you a living year.

געטרײַע זינד

מײַנע געטרײַע זינד,
איך האָב אײַך קיין מאָל נישט אמת געזינדיקט.
און אײַך קיין מאָל נישט געטאָן,
ווי מען טוט מעשׂים־טובֿים.
איך האָב אײַך תּמיד אָפּגעפּרעפּלט ווי אַ חובֿ,
איר האָט מיך קיין מאָל נישט דורכגעדרונגען,
דורכגערייצט ביזן ביין,
ווי מיצוות וואָס זייער זין
פֿלאַטערט אין געדעכעניש
ווי אַ גוטער, ווײַניקער פּסוק.

געבענטשט זאָלן זײַן די ליבע אויגן,
וואָס האָבן מיר פֿאַרמיצווהט
שטיקער רוי לעבן, שטיקער גראָז,
וואָס אויף זיי רוט איצטער מײַן קאָפּ
און חלומט שאַרפֿע חלומות.

באַשערט ביסטו מיר געווען.
געבענטשט ביסטו מיר געווען.

Loyal Sins

My loyal sins,
I've never really committed you
and never even done you
as one does good deeds.
I've mumbled you off dutifully,
you never even penetrated me,
teased me to the bone
like good deeds that
flap in the memory
like a fine apt proverb.

Blessings on your dear eyes
that have good-deeded me
pieces of raw life, pieces of grass
where I now rest my head
and dream sharp dreams.

You're my fate.
My blessing.

אין אַ געטאָ

אין אַ געטאָ פֿון טעג און נעכט
ליגט אונדזער אָפּגעראַטעוועט לעבן,
אַלץ וואָס טרעפֿט אונדז,
באַשערט און געגעבן,
איז ייִדיש דורך און דורך.
מיר האַנדלען דורך די טעג
מיט לײַען און באָרגן
און דרייען אַרײַן
די בײַנאַכטיקע, דערשראָקענע לאָמפּן
פֿון אונדזערע באַזונדערע זאָרגן.
פֿאַרפֿאַלן, ייִדישער פּאָעט,
נישט דיר איז באַשערט צו ווערן
אַ פֿעסטונג פֿון ציטאַטן.
דעם תּנך, וואָס זיי האָבן דיר צוריקגעוואָרפֿן
אַריבער דעם פּאַרקן,
האָב איך שוין לאַנג אויפֿגעהויבן אַ געשמדטן.
איצט ביסטו שוין ווידער אַליין.

אַליין.

פּאָעט, נעם די שטילסטע ייִדישע רייד,
פֿאַרגלייב זיי, פֿאַרהייליק אויף דאָס נײַ.
אַלע דײַנע מיצוות הויערן בײַ דײַנע פֿיס געטרײַ
ווי צוגעטרויטע קעצלעך;
קוקן דיר אין די אויגן,
זאָלסט זיי גלעטן און טאָן.
ווייסט גאָר ניט, ווי ס׳שטייט אַלץ אין קאָן.

זאָלסט זיי טאָן.

In a Ghetto

In a days-and-nights ghetto
our rescued life is lying,
everything that happens,
fated and accomplished,
is Jewish through and through.
We haggle away our days,
borrowing and lending,
then we turn on
the frightened nighttime lamps
of our lone burdens.
Too bad, Yiddish poet,
you're not fated to become
a fortress of quotations.
The Old Testament that they threw back at you
over the fence
I picked up long ago, already converted.
Now you're alone again.

Alone.

Poet, take the faintest Yiddish speech,
fill it with faith, make it holy again.
All your virtuous deeds huddle at your feet
like trusting kittens;
they look in your eyes
so you'll stroke them and fulfill them.
You don't realize everything's at stake.

So you'll fulfill them.

זײַ אָפּגעהיט. די פֿאַרוויסטונג רופֿט ווידער.
אַ ווילדער אַקער צעמורשט אַ גרויסע זעט
און געפֿינט דאָס האַרץ פֿון אַ סקעלעט.
און טאָמער זאָלסטו דיר אײַנרעדן,
אַז אַ סקעלעט איז אָן אַ האַרץ,
זאָלסטו וויסן, קראַנק ייִנגל,
דאָס גאַנצע צעגליטע,
צעצונדענע לעבן
אויף יענער זײַט פּאַרקן
קאָן דיך נישט שטאַרקן, דערהייבן,
ווײַל ס׳איז סקעלעטן־האַרץ
מיט דער גאַנצער פֿרייד,
רחמנות און גלאָקן פֿון גלויבן.

פּאָעט, וואָס פֿון דער נאַכט?
אונדזער באַפֿרײַונג איז קליין,
אומבאַוואַכט, אומבאַשיצט,
ווער דער שומר, באַוואַך,
פֿאַרוואָר —
דאָס בטחונדיקע טיר־און־טויער־געזאַנג
פֿון אַן איבעראַיאָר,
וואָס איז אויף תּמיד
אין דײַנע גלייביקע ביינער אײַנגעקריצט.

Be on guard. The wasteland calls again.
A wild plow grinds a great surfeit to dust
and finds a skeleton's heart.
And if you can talk yourself into believing
that a skeleton has no heart,
then you must know, sick boy,
that the whole glowing
incandescent life
on the other side of the fence
can't strengthen you, can't exalt you
because it's a skeleton-heart
with all its joy,
pity and chimes of faith.

Poet, what of the night?
Our liberation is tiny,
unguarded, unprotected.
Become the watchman; guard,
preserve—
this believing-hoping happily-ever-after myth
of a next year,
which is forever,
is bitten into your believing bones.

ווי מידע ביימער

די נאַקעטע חווה האָט מיט מיר געטיילט
דעם לעצטן ביס פֿון עפּל.
אַ פֿאַרשעמטער האָט גאָט זיך פֿאַרשטעלט
פֿאַר אַן עלעקטריש קנעפּל.
איך האָב עס געגעבן אַ באַריר,
ס׳איז געוואָרן ליכטיק
צווישן מיר און איר.

געבענטשט זאָלסטו זײַן,
האָב איך איר געזאָגט.
כ׳האָב פֿאַרחלומט אין זיך אַ מידער
אַן איינציקע רגע,
מיט אַזוי פֿיל ערשטיקן טונקל
אין מײַנע גלידער,
פֿון אוצר פֿון יענע געציילטע טעג,
וואָס האָבן זיך ביסלעכווײַז גענומען זאַמלען
מיט יעדער טריט אויף אונדזער וועג
אין שטיקער צײַט;
פֿון יענע נאָגנדיקע שטאַמלען,
וואָס זענען געוואָרן באַטײַט.
דערמאָנסט זיך?

דערמאָנסט זיך,
ווי מיר האָבן זיך געפּעדערט
און געקומען יונגערהייט,
אָבער גאָט האָט שוין פֿאַר אונדז
אַלץ געהאַט צוגעגרייט.
ווי פֿרי מיר זענען געקומען,
איז ער געקומען אַ ביסל פֿריִער.
מיר האָבן תּמיד געפֿרעגט:
ווער איז געווען ערשט, ער צי מיר?

Like Weary Trees

Naked Eve shared the last bite
of the apple with me.
God, bashful, disguised himself
as an electric button.
I touched it
and where was light
between her and me.

Blessings on you,
I said to her.
Wearily, with my limbs
full of first darkness,
I dreamed of a
single moment
out of the treasure of those numbered days
that, with every step of the way,
slowly gathered
into pieces of time; dreamed
of those crude stammerings
that became eloquence.
Do you remember?

Do you remember
how we rose early
and came, in our newness,
but God had already prepared
everything for us?
No matter how early we came,
he came a little earlier.
We always asked:
Who was first, he or we?

מיר האָבן שוין געהאַט
אַ גאַנצן וואַלד מיט זינגענדיקע פֿייגל,
שטאַרקע חיות און געטרײַע ליכט.
און אַלע מאָל איז ער צווישן אונדז
אויסגעוואַקסן אומגעריכט.

דערמאָנסט זיך?
מיר זענען געזעסן אויף דער ערד,
געגעסן די ערשטע פֿרוכט פֿון שוויס.
געפּלאַפּלט. אַ פֿאַרדרימלטער
האָט ער זיך צוגעהערט.
ס'איז געווען קוים, אָקערשט ערשט,
ס'איז זיך נאָך גאָרניט פֿאַרלאָפֿן.
ווי מידעביימער זענען מיר
איינער אין אַנדערן
שטענדיק אַרײַנגעשלאָפֿן.

We already had
a whole forest of singing birds,
strong beasts, faithful light.
And all the time he kept turning up
unexpectedly between us.

Do you remember?
We sat on the ground,
ate the first fruit of our sweat.
Prattled. Drowsily
he listened.
It was just barely first,
nothing had yet happened.
Like weary trees,
interlaced,
shadowy we fell asleep.

די פֿרייד פֿון ייִדישן וואָרט

.3

אַ לאָזט מיך צו צו דער פֿרייד פֿון ייִדישן וואָרט.
גיט מיר גאַנצע, פֿולע מעת־לעתן.
פֿאַרקניפּט מיך, פֿאַרוועבט מיך,
טוט מיך אויס פֿון אַלע אייטלקייטן.
באַשפּײַזט מיך דורך קראָען, שענקט מיר קרישקעס,
אַ געלעכערטן דאַך און אַ האַרט בעט.
אָבער גיט מיר גאַנצע, פֿולע מעת־לעתן,
לאָזט מיך נישט דאָס ייִדישע וואָרט
אויף אַ רגע פֿאַרגעסן.

איך ווער שטרענג און געביטעריש
ווי די האַנט פֿון מײַן פּרנסה.
די קאַפּהענער און דער שאַמפּאַניער
אומפֿאַרדייען מײַן צײַט.
דאָס ייִדישע וואָרט ליגט פֿאַרשפּײַכלערט,
דער שליסל זשאַווערט אין מײַן האַנט.
מײַן מיושבֿדיקער טאָג רויבט מײַן פֿאַרשטאַנד.

אַ זינג, דערזינג זיך צו נאַקעטער קנאַפּקייט.
די וועלט ווערט פֿעט אויף דײַן געלעגער.
פֿאַר אײַך ביידן איז באַלד קיין אָרט נישטאָ.
דאָס ייִדישע וואָרט וואַרט אויף דיר געטרײַ און שטום.
און דו זיפֿצסט אין געצונדענעם חלום:
איך קום, איך קום.

The Joy of the Yiddish Word

3.
O let me come close to the joy of the Yiddish word.
Give me whole days and nights of it.
Bind me, weave me into it,
strip me of all vanities.
Let ravens feed me, I'll live on crumbs.
A broken roof, a hard bed.
But give me whole days and nights of it.
Don't let me forget the Yiddish word
for a single moment.

I'm becoming harsh and commanding,
like the hand of my livelihood.
Capons and champagne
indigest my time.
The Yiddish word lies garnered,
but the key rusts in my hand.
Logic steals away my understanding.

O sing, sing yourself towards naked austerity.
The world becomes fat in your bed.
There'll soon be no place for either of us.
The Yiddish word, loyal, silent, is waiting for you.
And you sigh in a burning dream:
I'm coming, I'm coming.

גלאַט אַזוי

האָט משה־לייב זיך אַנידערגעשטעלט
אין מיטן דער נאַכט, צו דערטראַכטן די וועלט.
הערט ער צום אייגענעם טראַכטן זיך אײַן —
שעפּטשעט אים עמעץ אין אויער אַרײַן,
אַז אַלצדינג איז גלײַך און אַז אַלצדינג איז קרום
און ס׳דרייט זיך די וועלט אַרום אַלצדינג אַרום.
צופּט משה־לייב מיט די נעגל אַ שטרוי
און שמייכלט.
פֿאַר וואָס? —
גלאַט אַזוי.

צופּט ער אַזוי זיך די שטרוי אין דער נאַכט,
טוט זיך אים נאָך אַ מאָל עפּעס אַ טראַכט.
טראַכט זיך אים — הערט ער זיך נאָך אַ מאָל אײַן —
שעפּטשעט אים עמעץ אין אויער אַרײַן,
אַז גאָרנישט איז גלײַך און אַז גאָרנישט איז קרום
און ס׳דרייט זיך די וועלט אַרום גאָרנישט אַרום.
צופּט משה־לייב מיט די נעגל די שטרוי
און שמייכלט.
פֿאַר וואָס? —
גלאַט אַזוי.

Just Because

Moyshe Leyb stood up
in the middle of the night to think out the world.
He listens to his own thinking—
someone whispers in his ear
that everything is straight and everything is crooked
and that the world spins around everything.
Moyshe Leyb picks at a straw with his nails
and smiles.
Why?
Just because.

He picks at a straw in the night,
and then he has another thought.
He thinks—he listens again—
someone whispers in his ear
that nothing is straight and nothing is crooked
and that the world spins around nothing.
Moyshe Leyb picks at a straw with his nails
and smiles.
Why?
Just because.

גיי פֿאַרטרײַב זיי . . .

אַז ס׳קומען לײַט מיט בלאָטיקע און גרויסע פֿיס,
און פֿרעגן קיינעם ניט, און עפֿענען די טירן,
און נעמען אין דײַן הויז בײַ דיר אַרומשפּאַצירן
ווי אין אַ זונות־הויז ערגעץ אין אַ הינטערגאַס —
דאָ איז עס זיכער דאָך דעם האַרצנס שענסטער שפּאַס
אַ נעם צו טאָן אַ בײַטש אין האַנט, ווי אַ באַראָן
וואָס לערנט זײַנס אַ קנעכט גוט־מאָרגן זאָגן,
און פּשוט ווי די הינט זיי אַלע צו פֿאַריאָגן!

וואָס אָבער טוט מען מיט דער בײַטש, אַז ס׳קומען לײַט
מיט זאַנגען־בלאָנדע האָר און הימל־בלויע אויגן,
און קומען ווי די פֿייגל פֿלינק אַרײַנגעפֿלויגן,
און וויגן כּלומרשט דיך אין שיינע טרוימען אײַן,
און גנבֿענען דערווײַל זיך אין דײַן האַרץ אַרײַן,
און טוען זינגענדיק די קליינע שיכלעך אויס,
און באָדן, ווי אין זומערטײַכלעך קינדער קליינע,
בײַ דיר אין האַרצנס־בלוט די פֿיסלעך זיי׳רע שיינע?

Go Throw Them Out

When people come with big muddy feet
and open your door without a by-your-leave,
and begin to walk around inside your house
like in a whorehouse off in a back street—
then it's the heart's finest joke
to take a whip in your hand like a baron
teaching his servant how to say goodmorning,
and simply drive them all away like dogs!

But what do you do with the whip when people come
with corn-blond hair and heavenly blue eyes,
bursting in like birds briskly flying,
lullabying you as though with lovely dreams,
and meanwhile stealing into your heart,
singing, taking off their tiny shoes,
and, like children paddling in summer brooks,
dabble their pretty feet in your heart's blood?

Memento Mori

און אַז משה־לייב, דער פּאָעט, וועט דערציילן,
אַז ער האָט דעם טויט אויף די כוואַליעס געזען,
אַזוי ווי מען זעט זיך אַליין אין אַ שפּיגל,
און דאָס אין דער פֿרי גאָר, אַזוי אַרום צען —
צי וועט מען דאָס גלייבן משה־לייבן?

און אַז משה־לייב האָט דעם טויט פֿון דער ווײַטן
באַגריסט מיט אַ האַנט און געפֿרעגט ווי עס גייט?
און דווקא בעת ס׳האָבן מענטשן פֿיל טויזנט
אין וואַסער זיך ווילד מיט דעם לעבן געפֿרייט —
צי וועט מען דאָס גלייבן משה־לייבן?

און אַז משה־לייב וועט מיט טרערן זיך שווערן,
אַז ס׳האָט צו דעם טויט אים געצויגן אַזוי,
אַזוי ווי עס ציט אַ פֿאַרבענקטן אין אָוונט
צום פֿענצטער פֿון זײַנס אַ פֿאַרהייליקטער פֿרוי —
צי וועט מען דאָס גלייבן משה־לייבן?

און אַז משה־לייב וועט דעם טויט פֿאַר זיי מאָלן
ניט גרוי און ניט פֿינצטער, נאָר פֿאַרבנרײַך שיין,
אַזוי ווי ער האָט אַרום צען זיך באַוויזן
דאָרט ווײַט צווישן הימל און כוואַליעס אַליין —
צי וועט מען דאָס גלייבן משה־לייבן?

Memento Mori

And if Moyshe Leyb the poet should tell
that he saw death in the waves,
as one sees oneself in the mirror,
in the morning, of all times, around ten o'clock,
would they believe Moyshe Leyb?

And if Moyshe Leyb greeted death from a distance
with his hand, and asked, How's it going?
precisely at the moment when thousands of people
were having the time of their life in the water,
would they believe Moyshe Leyb?

And if Moyshe Leyb, weeping, should swear
that he was drawn to death as much
as a fellow mooning around in the evening
at the window of a lady he's made holy,
would they believe Moyshe Leyb?

And if Moyshe Leyb should picture death for them,
not gray and dark, but gorgeously colorful,
just as it showed itself around ten o'clock,
there, far away, between sky and wave, alone,
would they believe Moyshe Leyb?

כ׳בין דורכגעווייקט מיט דיר –

כ׳בין דורכגעווייקט מיט דיר, ווי ערד מיט פֿרילינגדיקן רעגן
און ס׳הענגט מײַן בלאָנדסטער טאָג
בײַם קלאַפּנדיקן דופֿק פֿון דײַן שטילסטן וואָרט,
ווי די בין בײַם צווײַג פֿון בליִענדיקע ליפּעס.

און כ׳בין איבער דיר, ווי דער צוזאָג פֿון שפֿע
אין דער צײַט,
ווען אין פֿעלד גלײַכט זיך אויס דער ווייץ מיטן קאָרן.

פֿון מײַנע שפּיצפֿינגער טריפֿט געטרײַשאַפֿט אויף דײַן מידן קאָפּ,
און מײַנע יאָרן,
ווי די בייטן אינעם פֿעלד,
ווערן צײַטיק־רײַף און אָנגעקוואָלן
פֿון צער
דיך צו ליבן, געליבטער מאַן.

RACHEL KORN

I'm Soaked Through with You

I'm soaked through with you, like earth with spring rain,
and my fairest day hangs
on the pulse of your quietest word,
like a bee near the branch of a flowering linden.

I'm over you like the promise of surfeit
in the time
when the wheat comes up even with the rye in the field.

From the tips of my fingers my devotion pours on your tired
  head
and my years
like sown acres
become timely ripe and gravid
with the pain
of loving you, beloved man.

אַ בריוו

ווייסט, ליבסטער –
הײַנט איז דער טאָג אַזוי זוניק און האַרב,
ווי אַ גאָלד־געלע פּרוכט.
איך וואָלט אים געצומען
פאַמעלעך און צערטלעך,
אַז כ׳זאָל נישט אָפּמעקן פֿון אים די קלאָרע פֿאַרב,
אײַנגעוויקלט אין דעם ווייכן פֿלאַקס פֿון מײַנע טרוימען
און געשיקט צו דיר,
ווי אַ בריוו.

נאָר כ׳ווייס,
אַז וואָלטסט דעם „בריוו" צוריקגעשיקט גאָר באַלד
מיט אַ ראַנד־באַמערקונג גאָר ציכטיק און פֿײַן,
אַז אָסור, דו פֿאַרשטייסט נישט, וואָס איך מיין
(עס איז דאָך, רחל, מיט דיר אַזוי אייביק, אייביק)
און ביסט גאָר בייז,
יאָ, בייז ביסטו אַפֿילו.
ווײַל דער קוווערט – איז ליידיק.

A Letter

You know, sweetheart—
today the day is as sunny and tart
as a yellow-gold fruit.
I'd like to take it
slowly and tenderly,
so as not to erase its translucent color,
and wrap it in the soft flax of my dreams
and send it to you
like a letter.

But I know
you'd send the "letter" back immediately
with a note on the margin, all neat and fine,
that, I swear, you don't understand what I mean
(it's always like this with you, Rachel, always)
and you're angry,
yes, you're even angry.
Because the envelope—is empty.

בענקשאַפֿט

ס׳זענען מײַנע חלומות אַזוי פֿול מיט בענקשאַפֿט,
אַז ס׳שמעקט אַיעדן אינדערפֿרי
מײַן לײַב מיט דיר –
און ס׳טרינקט צו פּאַמעלעך אויף מײַן צײַנפֿאַרקלעמטער ליפּ
דער אײנציקער סימן פֿון דערשטיקטן טרויער,
אַ טראָפּן בלוט.

און ס׳גיסן שוין איבער די שעהען, ווי כּוסות,
אײנע אין דער צווייטער,
די האָפֿענונג, ווי טײַערן ווײַן –
אַז דו ביסט נישט ווײַט,
אַז אָט, אַיעדע רגע
קענסטו קומען, קומען, קומען.

Longing

My dreams are so full of longing
that every morning
my body smells of you—
and on my bitten lip there slowly dries
the only sign of suffering,
a speck of blood.

And the hours like goblets pour hope,
one into the other,
like expensive wine:
that you're not far away,
that now, at any moment,
you may come, come, come.

מײַן גוף

מײַן גוף איז נאָך ווי ביימערשטאָם אין וואַלד
געווענדט צו דער הייך מיט אַלע זײַנע גלידער,
די בענקשאַפֿט גרינט אויף ס'נײַ
מיט יעדער יונגער ליבע –

נאָר מײַן שאָטן,
ווי אַ שלייער
אויסגעוועבט פֿון דינסטן טרויער
נעמט שוין פֿון מײַן געשטאַלט די מאָס
פֿאַר וואַרטנדיקער ערד,
פֿאַר פֿײַכטן גראָז.

פֿירט דער זומערטאָג
אין רעם אַרײַנגעפּאַסט
פֿון שמאָלן שאָטנפּאַס,
און טונקעלער ווערט דאָס גראָז
בײַ מײַנע פֿיס,
גלײַך ס'וואָלט עס גראָד באַרירט
דער ערשטער הייך פֿון האַרבסט.

מײַן שאָטן,
ווי אַ שלייער
אויסגעוועבט פֿון דינסטן טרויער
נעמט שוין פֿון מײַן געשטאַלט
די מאָס
און פֿאַרשוועסטערט מיך
מיט וואַרטנדיקער ערד,
מיט פֿײַכטן גראָז –
און אין מײַן בלוט
הער איך וויינען די וועלט
און דאָס נישט־געבוירענע ליד.

My Body

My body's like a tree trunk in the woods—
it stretches to the sky with all its branches,
its longing greens again
with each young love—

But my shadow
like a veil
stitched of thinnest mourning,
already takes my measure
for waiting earth,
for moist grass.

The summer day turns icy
in the hoop
of the narrow cask of shadows,
and the grass darkens
at my feet,
as though it were just touched
by a first breath of autumn.

My shadow
like a veil
stitched of thinnest mourning
already takes
my measure
and sisters me
with waiting earth,
with moist grass—
and in my blood
I hear the world's weeping
and my unborn song.

May 1941

כ׳וויל צוגיין אַ מאָל

כ׳וויל צוגיין אַ מאָל,
אויף פֿינגערשפּיצן בלויז
צו אַ פֿרעמדן הויז
און מיט מײַנע הענט באַטאַפּן די ווענט –
פֿון וואָס פֿאַר אַ ליים עס זענען די ציגל געברענט,
פֿון וואָס פֿאַר אַ האָלץ די טיר איז געמאַכט,
און וואָס פֿאַר אַ גאָט האָט דאָרט זײַן געצעלט,
אַז ער האָט עס פֿון אומגליק און חורבן באַוואַכט?

וואָס פֿאַר אַ שוואַלב האָט אונטער זײַן דאַך
פֿון שטרוי און ערד געקלעבט זיך איר נעסט,
און וועלכע מלאכים פֿאַר מענטשן פֿאַרשטעלטע
עס זענען געקומען אַלס געסט?

וואָס פֿאַר אַ צדיקים האָבן זיי באַגעגנט
און שיסלען מיט וואַסער געטראָגן אַנטקעגן
אומצוּוואַשן דעם שטויב פֿון זייערע פֿיס,
דעם שטויב פֿון די ערדישע וועגן?

און וואָס פֿאַר אַ ברכה האָבן זיי געלאָזן
די קינדער – פֿון גרויס ביז מיזינקע,
אַז זי האָט זיי באַשערעמען געקענט און באַהיטן
פֿאַר בעלזשעץ, מײַדאַנעק, טרעבלינקע?

פֿון אַט אַזאַ הויז,
באַצוימט מיט באַמאָלטע שטאַכעטן,
אין מיטן פֿון ביימער און בלומיקע בייטן,
וואָס בלויען, גאָלדיקן, פֿלאַמען,
איז אַרויס –
דער מערדער פֿון מײַן פֿאָלק,
פֿון מײַן מאַמען.

Sometimes I Want to Go Up

Sometimes I want to go up
on tiptoe
to a strange house
and feel the walls with my hands—
what kind of clay is baked in the bricks,
what kind of wood is in the door,
and what kind of god has pitched his tent here,
to guard it from misfortune and ruin?

What kind of swallow under the roof
has built its nest from straw and earth,
and what kind of angels disguised as men
came here as guests?

What holy men came out to meet them,
bringing them basins of water
to wash the dust from their feet,
the dust of earthly roads?

And what blessing did they leave
the children—from big to small,
that it could protect and guard them
from Belzhets, Maidanek, Treblinka?

From just such a house,
fenced in with a painted railing,
in the middle of trees and blooming flowerbeds,
blue, gold, flame,
there came out—
the murderer of my people,
of my mother.

כ׳וועל לאָזן וואַקסן מײַן צער,
ווי שמשון אַ מאָל זײַנע האָר
און דרייען דעם מילשטיין פֿון טעג
אַרום יענער בלוטיקער שפּור.

ביז אַ מאָל, אין אַ נאַכט,
ווען כ׳וועל דערהערן איבער מיר
דעם מערדערס שיכּורן לאַך,
וועל איך אַ ריס טון פֿון אַנגלען די טיר
און אַ שאָקל מיט דעם געבײַ —
ס׳זאָל געבן די נאַכט אַ דערוואַך
פֿון שוידער, וואָס וועט אַדורך יעדע שויב,
יעדן ציגל און נאָגל און ברעט פֿונעם הויז,
פֿון סאַמע גרונט ביזן דאַך —

כאָטש כ׳וויס עס, וויס, מײַן האַר,
אַז ס׳וועלן די פֿאַלנדע ווענט
באַגראָבן בלויז מיך
און מײַן צער.

I'll let my sorrow grow
like Samson's hair long ago,
and I'll turn the millstone of days
around this bloody track.

Until one night
when I hear over me
the murderer's drunken laugh,
I'll tear the door from its hinges
and I'll rock the building—
till the night wakes up
from the shaking coming through every pane,
every brick, every nail, every board of the house,
from the very ground to the roof—

Although I know, I know, my God,
that the falling walls
will bury only me
and my sorrow.

Stockholm, 1947

אַ נײַ קלייד

איך האָב זיך אָנגעטון הײַנט
צום ערשטן מאָל
נאָך זיבן לאַנגע יאָר
אַ נײַ קלייד.

נאָר ס׳איז צו קורץ פֿאַר מײַן טרויער
און צו ענג פֿאַר מײַן לייד,
און ס׳איז אַיעדער ווײַס־גלעזערנער קנאָפּ,
ווי אַ טרער,
וואָס פֿליסט פֿון די פֿאַלדן אַראָפּ
פֿאַרשטיינערט און שווער.

A New Dress

Today for the first time
after seven long years
I put on
a new dress.

But it's too short for my grief,
too narrow for my sorrow,
and each white-glass button
like a tear
flows down the folds
heavy as a stone.

Stockholm, 1947

פֿון יענער זײַט ליד

פֿון יענער זײַט ליד איז אַ סאָד פֿאַראַן
און אין סאָד איז אַ הויז מיט אַ שטרויענעם דאַך –
עס שטייען דרײַ סאָסנעס און שווײַגן זיך אויס,
דרײַ שומרים אויף שטענדיקער וואַך.

פֿון יענער זײַט ליד איז אַ פֿויגל פֿאַראַן,
אַ פֿויגל ברוין־געל מיט אַ רויטלעכער ברוסט,
ער קומט דאָרט צו פֿליִען יעדן ווינטער אויף ס'נײַ
און הענגט, ווי אַ קנאָספּ אויף דעם נאַקעטן קוסט.

פֿון יענער זײַט ליד איז אַ סטעזשקע פֿאַראַן,
אַזוי שמאָל און שאַרף, ווי דער דין־דינסטער שניט,
און עמעץ, וואָס האָט זיך פֿאַרבלאָנדזשעט אין צײַט,
גייט דאָרט אום מיט שטילע און באָרוועסע טריט.

פֿון יענער זײַט ליד קענען וווּנדער געשען
נאָך הײַנט, אין אַ טאָג, וואָס איז כמאַרנע און גראָ,
ווען ער דופּקט אַרײַן אין דעם גלאָז פֿון דער שויב
די צעפּיבערטע בענקשאַפֿט פֿון אַ וווּנדיקער שעה.

פֿון יענער זײַט ליד קען מײַן מאַמע אַרויס,
און שטיין אויף דער שוועל אַ ווײַלע פֿאַרטראַכט
און מיך רופֿן אַהיים, ווי אַ מאָל, ווי אַ מאָל:
– גענוג זיך געשפּילט שוין, דו זעסט נישט? ס'איז נאַכט.

On the Other Side of the Poem

On the other side of the poem there's an orchard—
and in the orchard a house with a straw thatch;
three silent pine trees are standing there,
three guardians forever keeping watch.

On the other side of the poem there's a bird,
a brown-yellow bird with a reddish breast
that returns here every winter
and hangs like a bud on the naked bush.

On the other side of the poem there's a path
narrow and steep, the thinnest sliver,
and someone who's lost her way in time
comes, quiet, barefoot, to haunt me there.

On the other side of the poem there may be
a miracle. But today is dreary and gray;
a feverish longing for an amazing hour
flutters against my window pane.

On the other side of the poem my mother
stands on the threshhold, stands in thought,
and calls me home as of old, as of old:
You've played long enough! Can't you see it's night?

אַלץ וואָס איז איינזאַם

אַלץ, וואָס איז איינזאַם, האָט די פֿאַרב פֿון מײַן טרויער,
און אַלץ, וואָס פֿאַרשעמט איז און מיד,
שטייט אין אַ קרוין פֿון פֿאַרלאָשענע שטערן
בײַ דעם ערשטן וואָרט פֿון מײַן ליד.

פֿאַרוואָרלאָזטע בעטלער, פֿאַרשטויסענע פּרינצן,
פֿאַרגעסענער שמייכל, פֿאַרשפּעטיקט געוויין —
ווער וועט זיך נייגן פֿאַר אײַך און פֿאַרבעטן
אײַך אַלע, ווען איך וועל נישט זײַן?

Everything Forlorn

Everything forlorn wears the color of my grief.
Everything ashamed and weary
lives in a crown of extinguished stars
beside the first word of my poem.

Outcast beggars, exiled princes,
forgotten smiles, too-late laments,
who will bow before you and invite
you in, when I no longer am?

גיי איך מיר אַזוי אַרום, אַרום, אַרום

גיי איך מיר אַזוי אַרום, אַרום, אַרום
אַ יאָר און צוויי, און דריַי, און ס'קאָן זײַן מער;
איך קום אַזוי זיך, ניט געבעטן, אומעטום, אומעטום,
און אומעטום איז וויסט און לער . . .

ס'איז וויסט און לער,
און אומעטיק,
און נודנע שווער,
בררו! . . .

MOYSHE KULBAK

I Just Walk Around, Around, Around

I just walk around, around, around
for a year, and two, and three, and maybe more;
I arrive uninvited everywhere, everywhere,
and everywhere it's void and empty . . .

It's void and empty,
and lonely,
and terribly boring,
brrr! . . .

װעסנעדיקס

ס׳ליגן ברײט, ס׳ליגן גרויס מײַנע באָרװעסע טריט
אויף דעם פֿעלד, אויף דעם שװאַרצן.
ס׳איז מײַן לײַב אָט די ערד. כ׳בין אַ ראָזעװע ליד
פֿון איר האַרצן.

שטראָמיק כליופּעט מײַן הונגעריקער גאַנג אין דער פֿרי.
כ׳שפּרײט פֿונאַנדער די הענט
טראַלאַלאַ, טראַלאַלאַ!
ס׳האָט די שטראַליקע װעלט ניט קײן װענט.

הײ, אַהינטער די פֿיס, װאָס צעטרעטן מיר,
אַ לויב צו דעם שיכּורן לעבן ---
איך שפּרײַז און איך לאַך אין אַיעטװידער טיר:
האָט איר גאָרניט געזען?
האָט איר גאָרניט געהערט?
ס׳האָט די װעלט זיך מיר אונטערגעגעבן . . .

Spring

My barefoot steps lie broad and big
on the field, on the black field.
My flesh is the earth, I'm the ryebread-song
in its heart.

My hungry walk inundates the morning.
I spread my arms:
tra-la-la, tra-la-la!
The luminous world has no walls.

Hey, down with the feet that trample me,
hurray for the drunken life . . .
I strut and laugh into every door:
Haven't you seen anything?
Haven't you heard anything?
The world has surrendered to me.

זומער

הײַנט האָט די וועלט זיך אויפֿגעוויקלט ווידער נײַ;
דער גראָבער קנאָספּ, די פֿולע ערד, די גרינע שושקערײַ –
ס׳האָט אַלץ געציטערט, ווי אַ שטײַפֿער מיידללײַב
פֿאַרציטערט ווערט פֿון שאַרפֿער פֿרייד בײַם ווערן ווײַב . . .

און איך בין, ווי אַ קאַץ, געלעגן אויפֿן מיט פֿון פֿעלד,
ווּ ס׳האָט געשפריצט, געבליצט, געפֿינקלט און געהעלט,
איין אויג פֿאַרשמירט מיט זון, דאָס צווייטע – צוגעמאַכט,
כ׳האָב שווײַגנדיק געקוואָלן, שווײַגנדיק געלאַכט . . .
אַריבער מײַלן פליין, און וואַלד, און טאָל –
דאָ וואַלגער איך זיך אום – אַ בלאַנקער, האַרטער שטאָל.

Summer

Today the world unwrapped itself again,
fat bud, full earth, green whispering,
everything trembled the way taut girl flesh
trembles with the sharp joy of becoming a wife . . .

Like a cat I lay in the middle of the field
where it splashed, flashed, sparkled and glistened,
one eye smeared with sun, the other—closed,
and silently rejoiced, silently laughed . . .
over miles of plain and forest and valley—
here's where I lounge about—a splendid hard steel.

צווײ . . .

צווײ מענטשן, וואָס ווײנען אַ טיר לעם אַ טיר;
צווײ שכנים, צווײ בחורים הויכע, —
אַ מײדלדיקס אײנס און אַ בריאה אַ בלײכע
(אין מיר, אין מיר, אין מיר).
צווײ מענטשן, וואָס ווײנען אַ טיר לעם אַ טיר.

איך שלאָף. פּלוצלינג טשוכען זיך עמעצנס הענט . . .
(אַז אײנער גײט שלאָפֿן שטײט אויפֿעט דער צווײטער)
ער וויקלט פֿונאַנדער אַ שאָטנדיק־לײטער
און קריכט אויף די ווענט, אויף די ווענט, אויף די ווענט.
איך שלאָף. פּלוצלינג טשוכען זיך עמעצנס הענט.

און אַ מאָל, ווען מען זיצט בײַ אַ גלעזעלע ווײַן
(עס טרעפֿט, אוי, עס טרעפֿט, הלוואַי זאָל ניט טרעפֿן),
דאָס מענטשעלע טוט דאָן אַ טירל אַן עפֿן
און שפּײַט אין אַ פּנים אַרײַן . . .
אָ, אַ מאָל ווען מען זיצט בײַ אַ גלעזעלע ווײַן.

צווײ מענטשן, וואָס ווײנען אַ טיר לעם אַ טיר;
צווײ שכנים, צווײ בחורים הויכע, —
אַ מײדלדיקס אײנס און אַ בריאה אַ בלײכע
(אין מיר, אין מיר).
צווײ מענטשן, וואָס ווײנען אַ טיר לעם אַ טיר.

Two

Two people live side by side;
two neighbors, two tall boys,—
a girlish one and a pale creature
(in me, in me, in me).
Two people live side by side.

I'm asleep. Suddenly someone's hands start . . .
(when one goes to sleep, the other awakes)
he unrolls a shadowy ladder
and climbs up the walls, up the walls, up the walls.
I'm asleep. Suddenly someone's hands start.

Sometimes when I sit with a glass of wine
(it happens, it happens, if only it didn't),
the little man opens a tiny door
and spits in my face . . .
O, sometimes when I sit with a glass of wine.

Two people live side by side;
two neighbors, two tall boys,—
a girlish one and a pale creature
(in me, in me),
two people live side by side.

גלידער

אָ, ווי פֿיל זאָגן אונדז די גלידער פֿון אַ מענטשן! –
אַ האַנט, וואָס עמעץ לייגט אַזוי זיך אויף די קני,
אַ האַלדז, אַן אַקסל, וואָס דו האָסט באַגעגנט
אין רוישיקן קאַפֿע, אין טראַם, צי אין טעאַטער.
ווי אָפֿט מאָל טרייסלען אויף דאָס האַרץ אונדז ליפּן,
וואָס קומען אונדז אַנטקעגן אומגעריכטערהייט;
עס ריידן האָר און בײַכער, ס׳רעדן בליקן
אַזוינס וואָס ווערטער קענען ניט!
ווי מאַכן ציטערן דאָס האַרץ אונדז פֿיסלעך,
די לײַכטע פֿרויענפֿיס, וואָס שוועבן אָפֿט פֿאַרבײַ!
דאָך איך האָב ליב נאָר די וואָס זײַנען גראָב און אומגעלומפערט;
אָן גוטע־פֿרײַנד, אָן אַלטע בריוו דערמאָנען זיי,
און אויך אָן דער, וואָס שענקט אונדז אונדזער לעבן.

ZISHA LANDAU

Parts

A man's parts tell us such a lot!—
A hand someone puts on his knees, like this,
a neck, a shoulder that you notice
in a noisy café, in a bus, perhaps a theater.
How many times your heart is jolted by lips
you suddenly meet;
hair and bellies speak, glances speak,
things that words can't say!
How feet can shake your heart!
Light women's feet skimming by!
But I love those best that are thick and clumsy,
they remind me of good friends, old letters,
and of her who gave me my life.

איך האָב צו אײַך אַ גרויסע טובֿה, ברידער . . .

איך האָב צו אײַך אַ גרויסע טובֿה, ברידער . . .
עס האַנדלט, נעמלעך, זיך אין דעם, אַז איר
מיט אײַער טיפֿער חכמה און פֿאַרשטענדעניש,
זאָלט מיר דערקלערן צי איך בין גערעכט. —
כ'האָב לעצטנס, ברידער, אַ געפֿיל: פֿון אַלע ליפּן,
וואָס שטייען גרייטע אויף דער וועלט געקושט צו ווערן,
אָם זיסטן זײַנען די, וואָס זײַנען צוגעוועלקט צו ביסלעך,
וואָס זײַנען בלייך, צעקנייטשט און אָפּגעקראָכן. אין קורצן די,
וואָס זײַנען אויסגעקושט, צעקושט און דורכגעקושט געוואָרן.
אויף ווי פֿיל ס'קען אַ מענטש זײַן אייגן האַרץ באַגרײַפֿן,
שטאַמט דאָס געפֿיל אין מיר דערפֿון, וואָס איך
האַלט זיך בײַ מײַניקן: בײַ אונדזער שטאַנד און יאָרן
אין זעכצן־יעריק בלוט אַן אומזין: איך האָב ניט איין מאָל שוין פּרובירט
בײַם קין אַ זעכצן־יעריקס צו נעמען,
האָט דאָס אַזאַ מין צאַפּל אונטער מײַנע הענט געגעבן,
אַז ס'האָבן ציטערן די הענט מיר אָנגעהויבן,
ווי כ'וואָלט אַ מײַזל אָנגעהאַלטן בײַ דעם עקל.
אָ, ברידער מײַנע, עס וויל ניט אײַער ברודער פֿלאַטערן
אין אָנגעזיכט פֿון זײַן אַלטעגלעך ברויט!
דערפֿאַר ווענדט ער אַצינד זיך נאָך אַן עצה
צו אײַער טיפֿער חכמה און פֿאַרשטענדעניש.

I Have a Big Favor to Ask You, Brothers

I have a big favor to ask you, brothers . . .
Namely, it has to do with the fact that you
with your deep wisdom and understanding,
might tell me if I am right.—
Lately, brothers, I have a feeling: of all the lips
that stand ready in the world to be kissed,
the sweetest are those that are a little bit faded,
that are pale, crumpled, and discolored. In short, those
that are kissed out, kissed up, kissed through and through.
So far as a man can understand his own heart,
the feeling in me stems from my
sticking to my opinion: in our condition, in our years,
sixteen-year-old blood is nonsense: I've tried more than once
to take a sixteen-year-old by the chin
but it gave such a shudder in my hand
that my own hands began to shake
as though I were holding a little mouse by its tail.
O brothers of mine, your brother doesn't want to
risk his daily bread!
That's why he turns to you now for advice,
to your deep wisdom and understanding.

דינסטיק

צוויי הייסע גלעזער טיי מיט מילך האָב איך מיר אויסגעטרונקען,
אַ דרײַ־פֿיר צוויבאַק אויפֿגעגעסן;
דערנאָך בין איך אַ לאַנגע צײַט בײַם טיש געזעסן,
גערייכערט און געקוקט מיר אויף אַ נאָגל אין דער וואַנט,
פֿיר לידער איבערזעצט פֿון דײַטש,
אַ מידער אויף דער סאָפֿע זיך אַוועקגעלייגט,
אַרום דעם קאָפּ די הענט פֿאַרלייגט
און דרײַ מאָל צו דעם באַלקן אויסגעשפּיגן.
מיר איז געוואָרן שווער,
פֿאַר וואָס דער זומער איז פֿאַרגאַנגען.
איך וואָלט דאָך איצט שפּאַצירן מיר אין פּאַרק געגאַנגען,
צי גאָר אין שטוב געכאַפּט מיר פֿליגן.
און נאָך אַ מאָל האָב איך צום באַלקן דרײַ מאָל אויסגעשפּיגן,
און אַלע דרײַ מאָל ניט געטראָפֿן,
דערנאָך בין איך מיר אײַנגעשלאָפֿן.

Tuesday

I drank up two glasses of hot tea and milk,
ate up three or four zwieback:
then I sat at the table for a long time,
smoked and looked at a nail on the wall,
translated four poems from German
and lay down tired on the sofa,
put my hands behind my head
and spat three times up at the ceiling.
I felt heavy
because the summer was over.
Otherwise I'd now go for a walk in the park,
or even hang around the house catching flies.
Again I spat up at the ceiling three times,
and missed all three times,
then I fell asleep.

אַוודאי ווייס איך —

אַוודאי ווייס איך, הײַנט איז זונטיק
און מאָרגן וועט שוין מאָנטיק זײַן,
און נאָכן פֿרילינג קומט דער זומער,
און אונדזער אָרדענונג איז אַ שלעכטע,
און אין ניו־יאָרק ווינט אַפּאַטאַשו,
דער שטאָלץ פֿון פֿראַנקרײַך איז זשאָרעס.

איך ווייס אויך פֿילע סודות טיפֿע:
דער הערצאָג פֿון אַברוצי איז
קיין הערצאָג ניט. ר׳איז אונדזער גלײַכן,
און גייט זיך אָפֿט אין גאַס שפּאַצירן
אין שיינע טעג; דער מאַנטל אויף דער האַנט.

איך ווייס אויך: דאַרווין האָט געטראָפֿן,
קאָפּערניק איז געווען גערעכט,
דאָך בעסער פֿון דעם אַלעם ווייס איך:
איך
בין
אַ פֿאַרלאָרענער אויף אייביק.

Of Course I Know

Of course I know today is Sunday
and tomorrow will be Monday
and after spring comes summer
and our system is a bad one,
and in New York lives Opatoshu,
the pride of France is Jaures.

I also know many deep secrets:
the Duke of Abruzzi is
no duke. He's our equal,
and often goes walking down the street
on nice days; his coat over his arm.

I also know: Darwin guessed right,
Copernicus was right,
but best of all I know:
I
am
lost forever.

דאָס קליינע חזירל

דאָס קליינע חזירל האָט מיט דעם אָפּגעזעגטן מויל
אַ גראָב געטאָן אין אָפּפֿאַל טיף, אַז ס׳האָט אַ דאַמף זיך אויפֿגעהויבן.
און נאָך דעם האָט עס אָנגעשטעלט אויף מיר
צוויי מילדע, חנעוודיקע מאַנדלאויגן.
אַ וואַרעמקייט האָט דורכגעפֿלאָסן מיך, ווען איך
האָב צוגעקוקט ווי ס׳דרייט און דרייט זיך,
און ענדלעך דרייט עס אין אַ שפּיץ זיך אויס דאָס עקל זײַנס;
אָ, ווי פֿיל חן ליגט אין די חזרשע עקלעך!
אָ, ווי פֿיל צערטלעכקייט! אָ, ווי פֿיל רייץ און אומשולד!
ס׳איז רייצנדיק און חנעוודיק ווי יענער לאָק, וואָס אין מײַן יוגנט
האָט ניט איין שעה פֿון רו גערויבט בײַ מיר!
און צערטלעך איז עס און אַזוי אומשולדיק
ווי דינע פֿערזן, געטלעכער ווערלען!

The Little Pig

The little pig with its sawed off snout
dug so deeply into the garbage that steam rose up.
And then it examined me
with two mild charming almond eyes.
A warmth flowed through me when I
saw how it twirled and twirled
and finally twirled its little tail into a point.
O how much charm there lies in a pig's tail!
O how much tenderness, O how much grace and innocence!
It's as graceful and charming as that curl that in my youth
robbed me of more than one hour of rest!
And it's as tender and as innocent
as your lines, divine Verlaine!

ווי קומט אַהער?

ווי קומט אַהער אין קראַנקן־קאַמער
דער פֿילאָסאָף דער אַמסטערדאַמער?

איך קוק זיך אײַן — קיין צווייפֿל מער.
ס׳איז ער. ס׳איז ער.

די פֿולע ליפּן. די לאַנגע נאָז.
דער גאַנצער קאָפּ ווי אונטער גלאָז.

עס אָטעמט שווער זײַן קראַנקע ברוסט
אין אָפּטן איבעררײַס פֿון הוסט.

דרײַ הונדערט יאָר — ווי איין מינוט.
אויף ליפּ — אַ פֿרישער טראָפּן בלוט.

דרײַ הונדערט יאָר לבֿנהס שטראַלן
אויף קאָפּ און קישן פֿאַלן. פֿאַלן.

אָ, געטלעכער, איך ריר דיך אָן. —
וואַך אויף. שטיי אויף. דערקאָן.

H. LEIVICK

How Did He Get Here?
(Spinoza Cycle, No. 2)

How did he get into this sickroom,
the philosopher from Amsterdam?

I look at him—there's no uncertainty.
It's he, it's he.

The full lips. The long nose.
The whole head as though under glass.

His sick chest heaves, straining,
racked, racked, by fits of coughing.

Three hundred years—as though one minute.
A drop of blood dots his lip.

Three hundred years of moonlight fall
on his head and pillow. Fall.

Holy one, I touch your sleeve.
Wake up. Rise up. Recognize me.

צוויי מאָל צוויי איז פֿיר

די תּאווהדיקע פֿעל
פֿון גוף אַראָפּגעשיילט;
וואָס טוט מײַן ריינע זעל?
זי ציילט, זי ציילט.

צוויי מאָל צוויי איז – פֿיר,
איך מאָל איך איז – דו,
דו מאָל דו איז – מיר,
טויט מאָל טויט איז – רו.

אין מיזרח־זײַט מײַן קאָפּ,
די פֿיס אין מערבֿ־זײַט;
יאָג גיכער, שטיי נישט אָפּ, –
נאָענט מאָל נאָענט איז – ווײַט.

שאָרך בײַם טיר. – סטוק, סטוק. –
ס׳איז אָפֿן, קום אַרײַן, –
לויכט אויף אין לעצטן קוק, –
טויט מאָל טויט איז – זײַן.

Two Times Two Is Four
(Spinoza Cycle, No. 11)

My body's passion-hide
is stripped away. My pure
soul, what does she do?
She counts, she counts.

Two times two is—four,
I times I is—you,
you times you is—me,
death times death is—rest.

My head is in the east,
my feet are in the west;
drive quicker, don't get lost—
near times near is—far.

Tap the door.—Knock, knock.—
It's open, come right in,—
kindle the last look,—
death times death is—being.

אַ גאַנצע לאַנגע נאַכט

אַ גאַנצע לאַנגע נאַכט האָט שטורעמדיק גערעגנט,
דער אַלטער עפּלבוים האָט זיך געדרייט אין קעלט,
געקלאַפּט תּחנונימדיק אין ליַיוונטן געצעלט,
ווי ער וואָלט מיט זיַין טיפֿער עלטער זיך געזעגנט.
נאָר אין באַגינען, ווען דער מיזרח איז עק וועלט
אַרויס דער זון דער אויפֿגעשטאַנענער אַנטקעגן —
אַזוי האָט גליַיך דער בוים מיט שׂימחה זיי באַגעגנט,
ווי ס'וואָלט אויף אים קיין מינדעסט בלעטל נישט געפֿעלט.

און אין געצעלט איז, ווי אַן איַינגעכישופֿטער, אַ מענטש געשלאָפֿן,
און נישט דעם בוימס און נישט דעם רעגנס קלעפּ געהערט,
און אין דער פֿרי מיט אויגן נאָך אין שלאָף פֿאַרלאָפֿן,
באַטראַכט האָט ער די פֿרישע שטראָמען פֿון דער ערד,
און אויף זיַין קאָפּ, דורך אויפֿגעשטראַלטן נעפּל,
געפֿאַלן זיַינען מיט אַ הילך פֿרימאָרגן־עפּל.

Through the Whole Long Night

Through the whole long night the rain stormed down,
the old apple tree twisted with cold,
pounded for help on the canvas tent
as though saying goodbye to his deep old age.
But at dawn when the east on the world's edge
came face to face with the rising sun—
the tree came to meet it with instant joy,
as though his smallest leaf had not fallen away.

In the tent a man slept, as though under a spell—
not hearing the clatter of tree or rain,
and at dawn, his eyes still clogged with sleep,
he gazed at the fresh pools on the ground,
while over his head, through sun-streaked mist,
the morning apples clanged as they fell.

איינזאַם

קיינער ווייסט נישט, וואָס איך זאָג,
קיינער ווייסט נישט, וואָס איך וויל —
זיבן מײַזלעך מיט אַ מויז
שלאָפֿן אויפֿן דיל.

זיבן מײַזלעך מיט אַ מויז
זענען, דוכט זיך, אַכט —
טו איך אָן דעם קאַפּעליוש
און זאָג: „אַ גוטע נאַכט“.

טו איך אָן דעם קאַפּעליוש
און איך לאָז זיך גיין.
וווּ זשע גייט מען שפּעט בײַ נאַכט
איינינקער אַליין?

שטייט אַ שענק אין מיטן מאַרק,
ווינקט צו מיר: „דו יאָלד!
כ׳האָב אַ פֿעסעלע מיט ווײַן,
אַ פֿעסעלע מיט גאָלד“.

עפֿן שנעל איך אויף די טיר
און איך פֿאַל אַרײַן:
„אַ גוט יום־טובֿ אַלע אײַך,
ווער איר זאָלט נישט זײַן!“

קיינער ווייסט נישט, וואָס איך זאָג,
קיינער ווייסט נישט, וואָס איך וויל —
צוויי שיכּורים מיט אַ פֿלאַש
שלאָפֿן אויפֿן דיל.

ITZIK MANGER

Alone

Nobody knows what I say,
nobody knows what I need—
seven mice and a mouse
are on the floor asleep.

Seven mice and a mouse
I think make eight—
I put on my hat
and I say goodnight.

I put on my hat
and I start to go.
But where to go late at night?
All alone?

A bar in the market place
winks at me: "You fool!
I've a firkin of wine,
a firkin of gold."

Quickly I open
and fall through the door:
Greetings to all,
whoever you are!

Nobody knows what I say,
nobody knows what I need—
two drunkards and a bottle
are on the floor asleep.

צוויי שיכּורים מיט אַ פֿלאַש
זענען, דוכט זיך, דרײַ.
זײַן אַ פֿערטער דאָ אין שפּיל
לוינט זיך? – נישט כּדאַי.

טו איך אָן דעם קאַפּעליוש
און איך לאָז זיך גיין.
ווּ זשע גייט מען שפּעט בײַ נאַכט
איינינקער אַליין?

Two drunkards and a bottle
I think make three.
Shall I make a fourth?
Not me.

I put on my hat
and I start to go.
But where to go late at night?
All alone?

האַרבסט

סעפּטעמבער. דער ציגײַנער און די נאַכטיגאַל
ווייסן זיך נישט ווו אַהינצוטאָן.

אַ לבֿנה־גייער שלאָפֿט בײַם קילן טײַך,
פֿון אַלע חלומות אויסגעטאָן.

אָפֿעליאַ, קראַנקע אָפֿעליאַ!

די מידקייט אין אַ זײַדן שפּיצנהעמד
גלעט מיט די פֿינגער דאָס גראָע טאָל,

זי גלעט און זאָגט שפּרוכן און זי וועקט
דאָס בלאָע וווּנדער פֿון אַמאָל.

אָפֿעליאַ, קראַנקע אָפֿעליאַ!

די גרינע אויגן פֿון דער סעפּטעמבער־נאַכט
קוקן מיר דורך אַלע שויבן אָן.

אין די אויגן – געוויין פֿון ווילדע קעץ.
וואָס גייען אונדז די דאָזיקע אויגן אָן?

לאָמיר אַנטלויפֿן! ווו אַנטלויפֿט מען, ווו?
דער בלינדער לאַמטערן שטייט און וואַכט,
און די טירן און פֿענצטער זענען צו –

טו תּשובֿה, אָפֿעליאַ!

פֿון אַלאַדינס בלאָען כּישוף־לאַמטער
האָט זיך דאָס וווּנדער אָפּגעטאָן,

Autumn

September. The gypsy and the nightingale
don't know what to do with themselves.

A moonwalker sleeps near the cool river,
stripped of all his dreams.

Ophelia, sick Ophelia!

Weariness in a silk dressing gown
smooths the gray valley with her fingers.

She smooths and says incantations and wakes
the blue marvel of once upon a time.

Ophelia, sick Ophelia!

The green eyes of the September night
look wearily through the windowpanes.

In those eyes—cries of wild cats—
what are those eyes to us?

Let's run away. But where can we run?
The blind lantern stands and watches,
and the doors and windows are closed—

Repent, Ophelia!

This marvel took off
from Aladdin's magic blue lantern,

און דער ציגײַנער און די נאַכטיגאַל
ווײסן זיך נישט ווו אַהינצוטאָן –

און איציק מאַנגער שלאָפֿט אויפֿן האַרטן דיל
פֿון אַלע חלומות אויסגעטאָן.

and the gypsy and the nightingale
don't know what to do with themselves.

And Itzik Manger sleeps on the hard ground,
stripped of all his dreams.

אַבישג שרײַבט אַהיים אַ בריוו

אַבישג זיצט אין איר חדרל
און שרײַבט אַהיים אַ בריוו:
אַ גרוס דער טאַלעקע מיט שאָף –
זי שרײַבט און זיפֿצט אָפּ טיף.

אַ גרוס דער אַלטער מאַמעשי
און דעם אַלטן ליפּעבוים;
זי זעט די ביידע אַלטע־לײַט
אָפֿט מאָל אין איר טרוים.

אַ גרוס דעם שיינעם מילנערױנג,
וואָס אַרבעט אין דער מיל –
דעם פֿאַסטעך עוזר, איר זאָל זײַן
פֿאַר זײַן פֿײַפֿלשפּיל –

דער מלך דוד איז אַלט און פֿרוס
און זי אַליין איז „עט״,
זי איז דעם מלכס וואַרעמפֿלאַש
וואָס וואַרעמט אים דאָס בעט.

זי האָט געמיינט . . . נאָר מאַלע וואָס
אַ דאָרפֿיש מיידל מיינט . . .
זי האָט נישט איין מאָל אין די נעכט
איר גורל שטיל באַוויינט.

אמת, סע זאָגן קלוגע לײַט,
אַז זי טוט אַ ווילע זאַך.
זיי זאָגן איר אַפֿילו צו
אַ שורה אין תּנך.

Abishag Writes a Letter Home

Abishag sits in her room
and writes a letter home:
Greetings to the calves and sheep—
she writes, sighing deeply.

Greetings to her old mother
and the old linden tree;
she sees both old folk
in her dreams frequently.

Greet the handsome miller
who works in the mill—
and the shepherd Oizer, whose
piping she cherishes still.

King David is old and pious
and she herself is, "oh, well"—
She's the king's hotwater bottle
against the bedroom chill.

She thought—but who cares what
a village girl may think . . .
more than once at night
she softly mourned her fate.

True, wise people say
she's being charitable.
They even promise her
a line in the Bible.

אַ שורה פֿאַר איר יונגן לײַב
און פֿאַר אירע יונגע יאָר.
אַ שורה טינט אויף פּערגאַמענט
פֿאַר אַ גאַנצער וואָר.

אַבישג לייגט אַוועק די פּען,
איר האַרץ איז מאָדנע שווער,
פֿון אירע אויגן קאַפּעט, פֿאַלט
אויפֿן בריוו אַ טרער.

די טרער פֿאַרמעקט די „מאַמעשי”
און פֿאַרמעקט דעם „ליפּעבוים”
און אין אַ ווינקל כליפּעט שטיל
אַ צאַרטער מיידלטרוים.

A line for her young flesh,
the years of her youth.
A line of ink on parchment
for the whole long truth.

Abishag puts down her pen,
her heart is strangely bitter,
a tear drips from her eyes
and falls on the letter.

The tear erases "mother"
and erases "linden tree"
while girlish in a corner
a dream sobs tenderly.

רחל גייט צום ברונעם נאָך וואַסער

רחל שטייט בײַם שפּיגל און פֿלעכט
אירע לאַנגע שוואַרצע צעפּ,
הערט זי ווי דער טאַטע הוסט
און סאָפּעט אויף די טרעפּ.

לויפֿט זי גיך צום אַלקער צו:
„לאה! דער טאַטע! שנעל!"
לאה באַהאַלט דעם שונדראָמאַן
און ווײַזט זיך אויף דער שוועל.

דאָס פּנים בלייך און אויסגעצאַמט,
די אויגן רויט און פֿאַרוויינט.
„לאה, מאַכסט פֿון די אויגן אַ תּל,
געננוג שוין פֿאַר הײַנט געלייענט".

און רחל נעמט דעם וואַסערקרוג
און לאָזט זיך צום ברונעם גיין –
די דעמערונג איז בלאָ און מילד,
כאָטש נעם און און כאַפּ אַ וויין.

די גייט. און איבערן טונקעלן פֿעלד
בליצט שנעל פֿאַרבײַ אַ האָז.
– טשיריק! – אַ למד־וואָווניקל
טשיריקעט אין טיפֿן גראָז.

און אויפֿן הימל שעמערירט
אַן אוירינגל פֿון גאָלד:
„ווען ס'וואָלטן כאָטש געווען צוויי,
אײַ, וואָלט איך זיי געוואָלט".

Rachel Goes to the Well for Water

Rachel stands by the mirror and plaits
her long black braids,
she hears her father cough
and wheeze on the stairs.

She runs up to the windowseat:
"Leah! It's father! Quick!"
And Leah comes to the door,
hiding her trashy book.

Her face is drawn and ashen,
her eyes red and weepy.
"Leah, you'll ruin your eyes,
you've read enough today."

And Rachel takes the pitcher
and starts off towards the well—
the twilight is blue and mild,
it makes you want to cry.

As she crosses the dark field
a rabbit flashes by.
Chirik!—a little cricket
chirps in the deep grass.

And in the sky there shimmers
an earring made of gold:
"If only there were two,
I'd like to have them both."

אַ פֿײַפֿל פֿײַפֿלט אין דער נאָענט:
טרילי, טרילי, טרילי –
און ס׳שמעקט מיט דעמערונג און היי
פֿון אַלע שאָף און קי.

זי לויפֿט. שוין שפּעט. אין חומש שטייט:
בײַם ברונעם וואַרט אַ גאַסט,
די קאַץ האָט זיך געוואַשן הײַנט
און זי האָט הײַנט געפֿאַסט.

זי לויפֿט און ס׳פֿינקלט איבער איר
דאָס אוירינגל פֿון גאָלד:
ווען ס׳וואָלטן כאַטש געווען צוויי,
איי, וואָלט זי זיי געוואָלט.

A piper whistles near her:
tri-li, tri-li, tri-li—
The air is full of dusk and hay
from all the cows and sheep.

She runs. It's late. The Good Book says:
a guest waits near the well,
today the cat has washed her face,
today she fasted too.

She runs. And high up sparkles
the earring made of gold:
If only there were two,
she'd like to have them both.

איך בין געווען אַ מאָל אַ ייִנגלינג

איך בין געווען אַ מאָל אַ ייִנגלינג,
געהערט אין פאָרטיקאָס סאָקראַטן,
עס האָט מײַן בוזעמפֿרײַנד, מײַן ליבלינג,
געהאַט דעם שענסטן טאָרס אין אַטען.

געווען צעזאַר. און אַ העלע וועלט
געבויט פֿון מאַרמאָר, איך דער לעצטער,
און פֿאַר אַ ווײַב מיר אויסדערוויילט
מײַן שטאָלצע שוועסטער.

אין רויזנקראַנץ בײַם ווײַן ביז שפעט
געהערט אין הויכמוטיקן פֿרידן
וועגן שוואַכלינג פֿון נאַזאַרעט
און ווילדע מעשׂיות וועגן ייִדן.

ANNA MARGOLIN

I Once Was a Youth

I once was a youth
who listened in the arcades to Socrates.
I had a bosom friend, my beloved,
who possessed the most beautiful torso in Athens.

And then there was Caesar. Who built a glittering world
of marble. I was the last one left,
and my proud sister was elected
to be my wife.

Wearing wreaths of roses, drinking till all hours,
in peace and high spirits, I heard about
the pansy from Nazareth,
and the mad deeds of the Jews.

יאָרן

ווי פֿרויען, וועלכע זײַנען פֿיל געליבט און דאָך ניט זאַט,
און גייען דורכן לעבן מיט געלעכטער און מיט צאָרן
אין די אויגן זייערע פֿון פֿײַער און אַגאַט –
געווען אַזוי זײַנען די יאָרן.

און זײַנען אויך געווען ווי אַקטיאָרן,
וואָס שפּילן מיט אַ האַלב מויל „האַמלעט" פֿאַרן מאַרק;
ווי אין לאַנד, אַ שטאָלצן, גראַנסיניאָרן,
וואָס כאַפּן אָן דעם אויפֿשטאַנד פֿאַרן קאַרק.

און זע, ווי דעמוטיק זיי זײַנען איצט, מײַן גאָט,
און שטום ווי אַ צעשמעטערטער קלאַוויר,
און נעמען אָן פֿאַר ליב אַיעדנס שטויס און שפּאָט,
און זוכן דיך, ניט גלייבנדיק אין דיר.

Years

Like women who are loved very much and are still not sated,
who walk through life with laughter and anger,
and in their eyes shine fire and agate—
that's how our years were.

And they were like actors, playing
Hamlet out of the side of their mouths in the square;
like grandees in a land, a proud land,
who seize rebellion by the scruff of the neck.

But now see how submissive they are, my God,
as silent as a smashed piano,
and they take each blow and taunt as a caress,
and seek you, not believing in you.

לאַנגזאַם און ליכטיק

לאַנגזאַם און ליכטיק
האָסטו דײַן שווערן שטערן צוגעבויגן צו מײַן שטערן,
ביסטו פֿאַרזונקען מיט דײַן שוואַרצן פֿײַער
אין מײַן בלויען פֿײַער.

און מײַן צימער איז געוואָרן פֿול מיט זומער,
און מײַן צימער איז געוואָרן פֿול מיט נאַכט.
האָב איך מײַנע ליכטנדיקע, וויינענדיקע אויגן צוגעמאַכט,
האָב איך געוויינט שטיל אין מײַן שפּעטן זומער.

Unhurried and Radiant

Unhurried and radiant,
your forehead bent to my forehead
until your black fire sank into
my blue fire.

And my room filled with summer,
and my room became full of night.
I closed my light-filled, tear-filled eyes,
and wept silently in my late summer.

אוראַלטע מערדערין־נאַכט

אוראַלטע מערדערין־נאַכט, שוואַרצע מוטער אין נויט, העלף מיר!
פֿאַרנאַר אים, פֿאַרשפּין אים, פֿאַרשלינג אים, דערשלאָג אים צום טויט!

און איך,
וואָס טרערן זײַנען געווען מײַן געטראַנק,
און שאַנד מײַן ברויט,
וועל טרינקען פֿאַרחלשט,
גיריק און לאַנג,
ווי אַ ליבעס־געזאַנג,
זײַן ווײַבס געוויין,
דאָס שווײַגן פֿון קינדער,
דאָס פֿליסטערן פֿון פֿרײַנד
נאָך זײַן געביין.
וועל אויפֿשטיין ווי איינע, וואָס איז לאַנג געווען קראַנק,
אַ שוואַרץ געשפּענסט אין מאָרגנרויט,
וועל זיך בוקן צו אַלע פֿיר עקן פֿון רוים
און זינגען, און זינגען, און זינגען צום לעבן
אַ לויב פֿאַרן טויט.

Ancient Murderess Night

Ancient murderess night, black mother in need, help me!
Beguile him, entangle him, swallow him, beat him to death!

And I,
whose drink was tears,
whose bread was shame,
will drink swooning
greedily and long
like a lovesong
his wife's crying,
his children's silence,
his friends' whispering
over his corpse.
I'll get up like someone who's long been sick,
a black figure in morning-red,
and I'll bow to all four corners of space
and sing and sing and sing to life
my praise of death.

עפּיטאַף

דערציילט עס אים: זי האָט פֿאַרגעבן
זיך ניט געקענט איר טרויעריק געמיט,
איז זי געגאַנגען דורכן לעבן
מיט זיך אַנטשולדיקנדע טריט.

דערציילט, אַז זי האָט ביזן טויט
געשיצט געטרײַ מיט הוילע הענט
דאָס פֿײַער, וואָס איז איר געווען פֿאַרטרויט
און אין אייגענעם פֿײַער געברענט.

און ווי אין שעהען פֿון איבערמוט
האָט זי מיט גאָט זיך שווער געווערט,
ווי טיף געזונגען האָט דאָס בלוט,
ווי צווערגן האָבן זי צעשטערט.

Epitaph

Tell him this: she couldn't forgive herself
for her dark depressions.
She walked through her life
with apologetic steps.

Tell that until her death
she faithfully guarded the fire
entrusted to her, with pure hands,
and is burning in that same fire.

How in her hours of bravado
she battled hard with God,
how deeply her blood sang,
and how lightweights destroyed her.

אַ פֿרוי זאָגט:

האָסט דען ניט געזען עס אין זײַן בליק און גאַנג?
ער איז גרויזאַם און גרויס.
ער איז געפֿורעמט פֿון שטורעם.
די וועלט איז פֿאַר זײַן אימפּעטיקן גאַנג
אַ צו־ענג הויז.

און פֿאַר די שפּורן
פֿון זײַנע פֿלאַמענדיקע טריט
בין איך די טרויעריקע ערד, שוואַרץ און מיד.
זעסט ניט די וווּנדן פֿון די שאַרפֿע שפּורן?
אָבער אַ מאָל
בין איך פֿון קינדער־מעשׂהלעך דער הויכער טורעם
און שיץ אים, אַ דערשראָקענעם, פֿון שטורעם.

A Woman Speaks:

Have you noticed how he glowers and struts?
He's large and conceited.
He's created out of a thunderstorm.
The whole world's house is too narrow
for his quick stride.

And beneath the footprints
of his blazing steps
I am the sorrowful earth, black and weary.
Can you see the wounds from those sharp footprints?
But once upon a time
I was, as in a child's fairy tale, his highest tower
and refuge, when he was frightened by the storm.

פֿון פֿרויענלידער

צו דעם וועל איך קומען,
ווער ס׳האָט דער ערשטער מיר מײַן פֿרויענפֿרײַנד געבראַכט
און זאָגן: מאַן,
כ׳האָב נאָך איינעם מײַן שטילן בליק פֿאַרטרויט
און אין אַ נאַכט לעם אים מײַן קאָפּ געלייגט,
ערשט האָב איך מײַן צער,
ווי בינען אָנגעשטאָכענע אַרום מײַן האַרץ געבראַכט
און האָב קיין האָניק ניט אויף לינדערן מײַן וווּנד.
און ס׳וועט דער מאַן מיך נעמען פֿאַרן צאָפּ,
וועל איך אַנידערברעכן זיך אויף ביידע פֿיס
און בלײַבן אויפֿן שוועל ווי די פֿאַרשטיינערונג פֿון סדום,
איך וועל די הענט אַרויפֿהייבן צום קאָפּ,
ווי ס׳פֿלעגט מײַן מאַמע טאָן בײַם בענטשן ליכט,
נאָר ס׳וועלן מײַנע פֿינגער שטיין ווי צען געציילטע זינד.

KADYA MOLODOWSKY

FROM Women's Songs

I'll come to him
who first brought me my woman-joy
and say, Husband,
I've given my slow glance to someone else
and at night I laid my head beside him
and now I feel my guilt
like bees stinging around my broken heart
and I have no honey to soothe the wound.
And when my husband seizes me by the braid
I'll fall off my feet and lie on the threshhold
like those Sodomites turned to stone.
I'll raise my hands to my head
like my mother blessing the candles
but my fingers will stand stiff as ten numbered sins.

בײַנאַכטיקע געסט

בײַ נאַכט איז געקומען אַ פֿויגל צו מיר,
און געקלאַפּט מיט די פֿליגל,
אין מײַן פֿענצטער און טיר.
– קום אַרײַן, פֿויגל־פֿידל, גוטער קלעזמער פֿון מײַן יוגנטליד,
איך האָב ברויט נאָך און וואַסער פֿאַר דיר אָפּגעהיט,
קום אַרײַן, זײַ מײַן גאַסט, זײַ געערט.
ס׳איז אונדז ביידן דאָס לעבן און דאָס שטאַרבן באַשערט.

און אַ קאַץ איז געקומען פֿאַרבלאָנדזשעט פֿון נאַכט,
געדראַפּעט מיט נעגל,
געדראַפּעט, געשאַרט.
– קום אַרײַן, קיצל־קעצל, פֿון מײַן קינדהייט סטראַשנער ווילדטיר,
איך האָב ניט איין מאָל דעם בעזעם פֿאַרזוכט צוליב דיר.
קום אַרײַן, זײַ מײַן גאַסט, זײַ געערט,
ס׳איז אונדז ביידן צו בלאָנקען, נע־ונד זײַן באַשערט.

און אַ ציג איז געקומען, דאָס בערדל פֿאַרשפּיצט,
געקלאַפּט מיט די קלאָען,
מיט די הערנער געקריצט.
– קום אַרײַן, ציגל־מיגל, קורצע בערדל, מילך אין קריגל.
דײַן ליד נאָך ביז הײַנט מאַכט מײַן בעט פֿאַר אַ וויגל.
קום אַרײַן, זײַ מײַן גאַסט, זײַ געערט,
ס׳איז אונדז ביידן אַ מלמדישע דאָליע באַשערט.

בײַ נאַכט, אַ מענטש איז געקומען, זיך געשטעלט בײַ מײַן טיר,
און אַן אַנגסטיקע שרעק
איז געפֿאַלן אויף מיר.
– ווער ביסטו? צי דו טראָגסט ניט אַ מעסער אין האַנט?
צי דו טײַעסט פֿאַרראַט? צי דו טליִעסט אַ בראַנד?
און די טיר כ׳האָב פֿאַרשלאָסן, פֿאַרהאַקט און פֿאַרקלעמט,
און געפֿאַלן, דאָס פּנים פֿאַרדעקט מיט די הענט.

Night Visitors

One night a bird came to me
and knocked with its wings
on my window and door.
—Come in, feather-fiddle, kind musician of my child-song,
I've saved you some water and bread,
come in, be my guest, be honored.
We're both destined to live and to die.

And a cat came, wandering in the night,
scratched with its claws,
scratched and scraped.
—Come in, kit-kat, frightful beast of my childhood,
I've often been spanked because of you.
Come in, be my guest, be honored.
We're both vagabonds destined to roam.

And a nanny-goat came, with its pointed beard.
It knocked with its hoofs,
scratched with its horns.
—Come in, nanny-granny, short-beard, milk-in-mug.
Your song still makes a cradle of my bed.
Come in, be my guest, be honored.
We're both destined to teach for a living.

One night a man stood at my door,
and a terrible fear
took hold of me.
—Who are you? Is that a knife in your hand?
Are you a betrayer? A firebrand?
And I locked and barred and bolted the door,
and fell, hiding my face in my hands.

איז די נאַכט געווען פֿינצטער, אַזוי פֿינצטער, אַזש בלינד.
און מײַן דיל איז געווען אַזוי האַרט, ווי אַ שטיין,
און פֿון יענער זײַט טיר איז געשטאַנען דער מענטש,
און פֿון יענער זײַט טיר כ׳האָב דערהערט אַ געוויין.

And the night was dark, almost blind.
And my floor became hard as a stone,
and outside the door the man was standing
and outside the door I heard him crying.

די מאַמע

די מאַמע אין גרינעם סוועטער גייט איבערן גאַס און גייט.
אלול הוידעט זיך דער ווינט,
טבֿת שנייט,
זון איבער די שויבן פסח רינט.
דער גרינער סוועטער גייט איבערן גאַס און גייט
שוין זומערן,
שוין ווינטערן,
שוין וויפֿל צײַט –
די גאַסן שווימען אין דער לאַנג און אין דער קרים,
דער הימל הוידעט זיך אַזוי ווי אַ האַמאַק,
און אַלע גאַסן,
אַלע פֿירן צום פּאַוויאַק.

דאָרט ווי אַ ווונד אַ קאַמער ברייט,
אַ קאַמער וויגט זיך טאָג און נאַכט;
אונטער די גרויע ווענט אַ טאָכטער זיצט פֿאַרמאַכט,
פֿאַרשלאָסן,
שטיל,
מיט אויפֿגעלייגטע הענט,
מיט שאַרפֿע הערן,
און זעגט די קראַטן מיטן בליק
און ציילט די שטערן.
אַרום די שטילקייט קלינגט,
עס בלענדט די ליידיקייט מיט ווײַסע שפּיזן.

דער גרינער סוועטער גייט איבערן גאַס און גייט.
אלול איז נישט נאַס,
און טבֿת איז נישט קאַלט,
און פסח איז קיין יום־טובֿ נישט.

דער הימל הוידעט זיך אַזוי ווי אַ האַמאַק,
און אַלע גאַסן,
אַלע פֿירן צום פּאַוויאַק.

The Mother

Wearing a green sweater, the mother paces, paces
along the street.
In Elul the wind comes and goes.
In Tebet it snows.
At Pesach the sun trickles over the windowpanes.
The green sweater paces, paces along the street.
Summers go by.
Winters go by.
Years go by.
The streets float before her, endless and twisting.
The sky swings like a hammock,
and all the streets,
all, lead to Paviak prison.

In that place a cell throbs like a sore,
a cell rocks day and night;
behind the gray walls her daughter sits, closed up,
locked in,
silenced,
with folded hands;
listening intently,
she saws the bars open with her gaze
and counts the stars.
The silence rings,
the white fangs of emptiness glisten.

The green sweater paces, paces along the street.
Elul is not wet,
and Tebet is not cold,
and Pesach is barely a holiday.

The sky swings like a hammock,
and all the streets,
all of them, lead to Paviak prison.

אין שטאַל פֿון לעבן

מײַן אָרעמער פּעגאַז גייט צו פֿוס.
אי ער, אי איך – מיר האָבן ביידע שוין פֿאַרגעסן שוועבן.
די וועלט איז זייער קליין,
עס טריקנט אויס דער ים.
איך האָב דעם ווילדן סוסל אײַנגעשפּאַנט אין שטאַל פֿון לעבן.
שלעפּן מיר זיך ביידע שפּאַן נאָך שפּאַן.

און ווער האָט אָפּגעשאָסן פֿליגלען זײַנע?
און ווער האָט אָפּגעגריזשעט שפּיץ פֿון פּען?
די זון פֿאַרגייט, די שויבן בלוטיק שײַנען.
אָט ענדיקט זיך די זון. אָט ענדיקט זיך מײַן זען.

קומט, שורות, שטעלט זיך אויס, גיט מיך אַ הויב.
איר זענט מײַן שוץ און אויך מײַנע באַפֿעלער.
איך קען ניט איבערגיין דעם צאָם פֿון שפּינוועבס און פֿון שטויב
און ס׳ווערט מײַן פֿעלד אַלץ טונקעלער און שמעלער.

וואָס טויג באַרימערײַ, וואָס טויג?
וואָס טויג אַ מעשׂה נאָך אַ מעשׂה קנעטן?
נישט שטיי, פּעגאַז, צו נאָנט לעם היי פֿון סטויג,
דו קענסט, חלילה, ווערן אַ חמור מיט עפּאָלעטן.

In Life's Stable

My poor Pegasus must go on foot.
Both he and I—we've clean forgotten how to fly.
The world is very small,
the sea is drying up.
I've tied up this wild pony in the stable of life.
Now both of us drag our feet.

Who shot away his wings?
Who gnawed the point off my pen?
The sun sinks down, the windowpanes shine bloody.
The sun comes to an end. My sight comes to an end.

Come, lines, arrange yourselves, raise me up.
You're my bodyguard, my generals.
I can't cross over this fence of webs and dust,
the whole field darkens, narrows.

What good is boasting, what good is it?
What's the good of kneading out story after story?
Pegasus, don't stand too close to your stack of hay.
God forbid, you might become a donkey with epaulets.

ווײַסע נאַכט

ווײַסע נאַכט, מײַן פֿרייד און ווײ,
ביסט ליכטיקער פֿון ליכטיקן באַגינען.
עס זעגלט אויף אַ ווײַסע שיף אויף איסט־בראָדוויי,
וווּ כ׳קען בײַ טאָג קיין זעגל נישט געפֿינען.

אַ שטילער שטערן דערלאַנגט מיר אַ בילעט,
אַ גילטיקער פֿאַר אַלע ימען,
און איך טו אָן מײַן אוראַלטן זשאַקעט
און צי אַוועק אויף נאַכט־פֿאַרטרויטע לאַנען.

וווּ פֿירסטו מיך, מײַן שיף?
ווער איז דער באַשטימער פֿון מײַן רײַזע?
איך קען נישט לייענען דײַן מאַפּע־היעראָגליף,
און די צייכנס פֿון דײַנע ווײַזערס.

איך בין אַ זעעוודיקע און אַ סגי־נהור,
איך ווער געפֿירט אויף וועג דײַנעם געהיימען,
פּאַק אײַן אין באַגאַזש מײַן קראַנץ פֿון טרויער
פֿון אַלע מײַנע אָפּגעפֿליקטע היימען.

פּאַק אײַן מײַנע פֿאַרברענטע טעפּלעך,
די צעקנאַקטע שטערצלעך, שערבלעך, שערבלעך,
פּאַק אײַן מײַן תּהו מיט די גאָלדבאַפּוצטע קנעפּלעך,
ווײַל תּהו איז אומשטערבלעך.

פּאַק אײַן דײַן בריוו מיט די פֿאַרשוווּנדענע אַדרעסן.
מיט קאַלטן גרויל זיי בריִען מײַנע אויגן.
זיי זענען אויסער יאָרן און מעת־לעתן
אין מײַן מאָרך און ביין אַרײַנגעזויגן.

White Night

White night, my joy and grief,
you're brighter than the brightest dawn.
A white ship sails on East Broadway,
although I can't see its sail by day.

A silent star hands me a ticket
good for passage on every ocean.
I'm going to wear my oldest jacket
and surrender to the faithful night.

My ship, where are you leading me?
Who is the pilot of my journey?
I can't read your map of hieroglyphs
or the meaning of your instruments.

I'm one who sees and doesn't see,
I travel in your secrets' wake.
Pack my trunk with the wreath of sorrow
from all my lost, uprooted homes.

Pack up all my scorched-out pots,
their cracked lids, crumpled, crumpled,
pack up my chaos with its golden buttons
because chaos is stylish forever.

Pack up the letters with their missing addresses.
They scald my eyes with icy fear.
They've lasted past years, past days and nights,
sucked deep into my brain and bone.

פּאַק איַין מיַין שאָטן וואָס איז שווערער פֿון מיַין גוף,
ער גייט נאָך מיר מיט אייביקער רגילות.
ס'איז יום־טובֿ אָדער וואָך, ס'איז בליִונג אָדער וועלק,
מיַין שאָטן קומט און שעפּטשעט מיר מגילות.

פֿיר מיך אין אַ לאַנד פֿון צוקער־לעקעך,
וווּ כּרובֿים זיצן מיט קינדערלעך און נאַשן.
דאָס איז פֿון מיַין דינגעניש דער העכסטער מקח.
דאָרט ברויזט דער יין־המשומר אין די פֿלאַשן.

גיב מיר אַ זופּ פֿון אים, אָט דאָ אויף איסט־בראָדוויי,
אין זכות פֿון ייִדן וואָס וויינען אין די חצותן.
איך בין אַן אַפּיקורס, נאָר איך וויין מיט זיי,
מיט זעלבער עצבֿות און פֿאַרדראָסן.

איך בין אַ שווערער פּאַסאַזשיר, מיַין שיף –
פּעק מיט יאָמער, שופֿרות מיט געקלאַגן.
צי אָן די זעגלען פֿון דער נאַכט ביז פֿולסטער טיף,
וויַיל דער טאָג קען מיך נישט טראָגן.

פֿיר מיך צו אַ לאַנד פֿון לינדער רו,
וווּ ציגן טראָגן מיצלעך און שפּילן אויף טראָמבאָנעס,
צו די וויַיסע לײַלעכער פֿון קדוש־ברוך־הוא,
נאָך נישט באַוואָלקנטע מיט יאָגד און מיט סכּנות.

פֿיר מיך . . . יע, פֿיר מיך . . . דו ווייסט דאָך מערער
וווּ עס ליגט דער בלויער ים פֿון רו.
ס'איז מיַין מידקייט פֿון דיַין טורעם שווערער,
און מיַין האַרץ פֿאַרשלײַדערט ערגעץ וווּ.

Pack up my shadow, heavier than flesh,
that follows, follows me endlessly.
Holiday or weekday, blooming or fading,
my shadow comes and whispers its tales.

Lead me to a land of honey cakes
Where cherubs and children nibble the sweets.
That's worth more to me than anything,
there where the old wine sparkles in bottles.

Give me a sip here on East Broadway
to honor the Jews crying at midnight.
I'm a heretic, but I weep with them,
feeling the same sadness and guilt.

I'm a heavy passenger, my ship—
packed with laments and wailing shofars.
Tie up night's sails as tight as you can
because the day can't carry me.

Lead me to a land of tranquillity
where goats wear caps and play trombones,
to the white bedsheets of The Blessed One,
where the dangerous hunter can't shadow me.

Lead me, yes, lead me—you know best
where the blue ocean of peace now lies.
I'm wearier than your tallest mast,
somewhere I've flung my heart away.

אין דער פֿרעמד

כ׳האָב גאַנצע נעכט – (איך פֿרעג נישט וויפֿל!)
געווען מיט לייד און טרוימען רײַך . . .
געבענקט נאָך דיר, ווי ס׳בענקט אַ שיפֿל
נאָך קילע וועלן פֿון דעם טײַך.

געבענקט אַזוי ווי נאָך אַ בלימל
דער טונקל וויכער פֿרויענלאָק;
ווי ס׳בענקט די בלויקייט פֿון דעם הימל
נאָך מעשׂיות ריטמישע פֿון גלאָק . . .
געבענקט, ווי ס׳בענקט אַ פּוסטער וויגל
נאָך וועמענס ציטערדיקן שלאָף
ווי ס׳בענקט נאָך אָפּשפּיגלונג דער שפּיגל,
ווי ס׳בענקט דער אָנהייב נאָכן סוף . . .

LEYB NAYDUS

In an Alien Place

For whole nights—(don't ask how many)
I was rich with suffering and dreams . . .
I longed for you as a sailboat longs
for the cool swell of the river.

I longed for you as a dark soft curl
of woman's hair longs for a flower,
as the blueness of the sky longs
for the rhythmic fables of bells.
Longed, as an empty cradle longs
for someone's tremulous sleep,
as the mirror longs for reflection,
as the beginning longs for the end.

אָפּט ווילט זיך לאָזן די שורות

אָפּט ווילט זיך לאָזן די שורות ניט געוויגן און ניט געמאָסטן,
ניט אַרײַנקוועטשן דאָס האַרץ אין יאַמב און אין כאָריי,
ס׳ווילט זיך ריידן מיט אַ לשון אַן איינפֿאַכן און אַ פּראָסטן,
און ניט שלייפֿן און ניט טאָקן מײַן גליק און וויי . . .

ס׳ווערט עפּעס ענג דער מישקל, זײַנע ד׳ אַמות,
פֿרײַ, ניט געצוימט, זאָלן די פֿערזן גיין,
קלאָרע און האַרציקע, ווי אַ בליק דער מאַמעס,
אומגעצוווּנגען־ווילדע, ווי דאָס לעבן אַליין.

ס׳וואַרפֿט אַראָפּ די מוזע די עלעגאַנטע שיכלעך, וואָס דריקן,
און, דערשפּירנדיק דעם נײַעם אומדערוואַרטעטן געפֿיל,
לויפֿט זי באָרוועס, פֿרײַ, מיט אַ ווילדן אַנטציקן,
און זינגט זיך אינטימע ניגונים, ווי זי אַליין וויל . . .

I Often Want to Let My Lines Go

I often want to let my lines go without beat, without measure,
without squeezing my heart into iamb or trochee,
I want to speak in a language that's simple, direct,
and not file down my joy and my pain.

And the meter's so tight, it's four ells long,
let my lines go free, let out the reins,
clear and candid as a mother's look,
unrestrained, wild as life itself.

The muse kicks off her dainty cramped shoes,
surprised by the new unexpected feeling,
she runs barefoot, free, with a wild delight,
and sings when she chooses, her own melodies.

צוועלף שורות וועגן סנה

איז וואָזשע וועט זײַן דער סוף מיט אונדז ביידן – גאָט?
וועסטו מיך טאַקע לאָזן שטאַרבן אָט אַזוי
און טאַקע מיר נישט אויסזאָגן דעם גרויסן סוד?

מוז איך טאַקע ווערן פֿריִער שטויב, וואָס איז גרוי, אַש, וואָס איז
שוואַרץ?
און דער גרויסער סוד, וואָס איז נענטער ווי מײַן העמד, ווי מײַן הויט,
וועט אַלץ בלײַבן סוד, כאָטש ר׳איז טיפֿער אין מיר ווי דאָס סאַמע
האַרץ?

האָב איך טאַקע אומזיסט אין די טעג געהאָפֿט, אין די נעכט
געוואַרט?
און דו וועסט ביז דער לעצטער רגע בלײַבן געטלעך־גרויזאָם און
האַרט?
דײַן פּנים טויב ווי שטומער שטיין, ווי קיזלשטיין
בלינד־אײַנגעשפּאַרט?

נישט אומזיסט איז איינער פֿון די טויזנט נעמען דײַנע – דאָרן,
דאָרן דו פֿון מײַן גײַסט און פֿלייש און ביין,
שטעכנדיק – נישט אויסצורײַסן, ברענענדיק – נישט אויסצולעשן,
אַ רגע נישט פֿאַרגעסן – אַן אייביקייט נישט צו פֿאַרשטיין.

MELECH RAVITCH

Twelve Lines About the Burning Bush

What's going to be the end for both of us—God?
Are you really going to let me die like this
and really not tell me the big secret?

Must I really become dust, gray dust, and ash, black ash,
while the secret, which is closer than my shirt, than my skin,
still remains secret, though it's deeper in me than my own
heart?

And was it really in vain that I hoped by day and waited by
night?
And will you, until the very last moment, remain godlike-
cruel and hard?
Your face deaf like dumb stone, like cement, blind-stubborn?

Not for nothing is one of your thousand names—thorn, you
thorn in my spirit and flesh and bone,
piercing me—I can't tear you out; burning me—I can't stamp
you out,
moment I can't forget, eternity I can't comprehend.

אַ ליד – שלעכט אָדער גוט – אַ זאַך –
מיט איין אַטריבוט פֿלאַך

(אַ ליד פֿאַר מענטשן פֿון לידערפֿאַך –
און אויך זיי וועלן נישט אַלע פֿאַרשטיין)

וואָס איז דען אַ ליד? אַ פֿלאַך שטיק פּאַפּיר
באַפּינטלט מיט אותיות אַן אַ שיעור,
און אָפּט נעמט מען אַזעלכענע לידער אַ סך
און מען בינדט זיי אין אַ בוך – און אַ בוך איז אויך פֿלאַך.

און דאָס לעבן, וואָס ליד באַזינגט, איז בולט און האָט פֿאָרמען אַן
    אַ שיעור.
האָט קלאַנג און באַוועגונג, און עס איז אין דיר און עס איז אויסער דיר,
אַ מאָל קאָנקאַוו ווי אַ טיפֿער טאָל און אַ מאָל קאָנוועקס ווי אַ
    פֿעלדזנשפּיץ,
און עס שטראָמט ווי ניאַגאַראַ, און עס קלינגט ווי דונער, און עס
    שפּריצט מיט ליכט ווי בליץ.

און דאָך איז די וועלט – אויף איר אַ שוואַרץ יאָר,
אַזוי שיין געמאַכט, אַז פֿאַרגעננגלעך און נאָך אַ מאָל פֿאַרגעננגלעך איז
    די לעבעדיקע וואָר,
און אַ ליד – בלויז אַ שטיקל פּאַפּיר, אַזוי ביינערלאָז ווייך און דערצו
    אַזוי פֿלאַך,
איז דווקא אַן אייביקע און אַ דויערנדיקע זאַך.

און אַלץ, וואָס איז בולט, האָט באַוועגונג אין זיך און אַרום זיך
    פֿיזיק,
קען נאָר דעמאָלט ווערן אייביק, ווען עס ווערט אויף אַ שטיק
פֿון אַ פֿלאַך־ווייך פּאַפּיר „פֿאַראייביקט“ אין אַ ליד ––
איז עס נישט צו פּלאַצן? – – און די בולטקייט, אַרום וועלכער
    דו האָסט דײַן לעבן אָפּגעמיט

A Poem—Good or Bad—A Thing—
With One Attribute—Flat

(Poem for people in the poetry-business—
and not even all of them will understand)

What's a poem? A flat piece of paper,
dotted with endless letters,
and you often take many such poems
and bind them into a book—and a book's flat too.

And the life the poem sings about projects and has endless
forms,
has sound and motion, and is in you and outside you,
sometimes concave like a deep valley, sometimes convex like a
mountain peak,
and it streams like Niagara, roars like thunder, flashes like
lightning.

Yet the world—a plague on it—
is made in such a way that the living truth fades away, fades
away,
but a poem—simply a piece of paper, boneless, soft, and flat
besides,
is indeed an eternal and lasting thing.

And everything that projects, moves within itself and around
its shape
can become eternal only when it's "eternalized"
into a poem on a piece of soft flat paper—
doesn't that make you burst?—and this projection around
which you led your life

ווערט אויסגעגלײַכט, אויסגעווייכט, אויסגעפֿלאַכט אויף פּאַפּיר --
און ערשט דעמאָלט קען עס שוין לעבן יאָרן אָן אַ שיעור.
משמעות, אַז גאָט־וועלט־מענטש, אָט אָ די אָ דרײַ־איינציקע זאַך
האָט ליב אין דער פֿלאַך צו פֿאַרגיין. און וואָס קען שוין זײַן פֿלאַכער,
ווי אַ ליד איז פֿלאַך.

becomes straightened out, softened out, flattened out on
paper—
and only then can it live endless years.
It seems that god-world-man, this three-in-one thing
likes to pass into flatness. And what can be flatter than a flat
poem?

אויף מײַן װאַנדערפֿײַפֿל

אַ באָרװעסער װאַנדראָװניק אויף אַ שטײן
אין אָונטגאָלד,
װאַרפֿט פֿון זיך אַראָפּ דעם שטויב פֿון װעלט.
פֿון װאַלד אַרויס
דערלאַנגט אַ פֿלי אַ פֿויגל
און טוט אַ כאַפּ דאָס לעצטע שטיקל זון.

אַ װערבע פּאַזע טײַך איז אויך פֿאַראַן.

אַ װעג.
אַ פֿעלד.
אַ צאַפּלדיקע לאָנקע.
געהײמע טריט
פֿון הונגעריקע װאָלקנס.
װוּ זענען די הענט, װאָס שאַפֿן װוּנדער?

אַ לעבעדיקע פֿידל איז אויך פֿאַראַן.

איז װאָס זשע בלײַבט צו טאָן אין אָט דער שעה,
אָ, װעלט מײַנע אין טױזנט פֿאַרבן! –
סײַדן,
צונױפֿקלײַבן אין טאָרבע פֿונעם װינט
די רױטע שײנקײט
און ברענגען עס אַהײם אױף אָונטברױט.

און עלנט װי אַ באַרג איז אויך פֿאַראַן.

ABRAHAM SUTZKEVER

ON MY WANDERING FLUTE

A barefoot tramp on a stone
in evening-gold
brushes the dust of the world away.
A bird in flight
darts out of the wood
and grabs the last tatter of sun.

And there's a willow near a pond.

A path.
A field.
A trembling meadow.
Hidden footprints
of hungry clouds.
Where are the hands that make miracles?

And there's a fiddle that's alive.

What can I do in such an hour,
O my thousand-colored world—
except
gather this red beauty
into the wind's purse
and bring it home for supper.

And there's desolation like a mountain.

טאַנצליד

איך בעט דיך, קינד, צום טאַנץ. דו גייסט. און מיט מײַן בלאָנדן קאָפּ
פֿאַרנייג איך זיך אין טיפֿן זשעסט ביז צו דער ערד אַראָפּ.
און אָט אַזוי ווי כ׳קוק דיך אָן מיט אויסטערלישן גלי:
דײַן בייגעוודיקע זאַנגיקייט, דײַן אָרעס, דײַן קני,
די זינגעוודיקע ליניעס דורך דײַן הימלבלאָען קלייד
און מערער נאָך: די אויגן דײַנע – סאַמעטענע פֿרייד –
פֿאַרגעס איך ווו איך בין. איך ווער אַ פֿרילינגדיקער שטראַם
און זינג צו דיר אַרויס מײַן האַרץ דורך איטלעכן אָטעם
פֿון בלוט מײַנעס. דערנאָך, דערנאָך – און דאָס איז אַזוי עכט –
פֿאַרפֿלעכטן זיך די הענט בײַ אונדז און ביידע
זענען מיר אין אונדזער טאַנץ גערעכט.

און מיט אַ מאָל מיר גיבן זיך אַ שטורעמדיקן טראָג
דורך גרויסע וועלדער טונקעלע – אַריבער נאַכט און טאָג,
אַריבער צײַט. די וועלט באַהאַלט זיך אין אַ ווינקל ווו.
איך ווייס ניט ווער איך בין. מיר דאַכט: בין אָוונטגאָלד, בין דו,
צי גאָר אַ שוואַלב . . . עס פֿליִען נאָך געשרייען, טײַכן, שטעט
און אַלץ – אין אונדזער טאַנץ, דורך פֿאַרבן רויט און פֿיאָלעט
און גרין. דו וויינסט. איך הער. דײַן אָנבליק פֿאַלט אויף מיר ווי
פֿלאַם.
מיר דאַכט, דו ביסט אַ זעגלשיפֿל ערגעץ אויף אַ ים
און איך – אַ ווינט אַ זאַלציקער, מיט דיר אין אַ געפֿעכט.
דו ראַנגלסט זיך. איך פּאַטש מיט שוים. און ביידע
זענען מיר אין אונדזער טאַנץ גערעכט.

Song for a Dance

I invite you, child, to dance. You come. I bow my blond head,
bending it down to the ground.
Eager, warm, this is how I see you:
a yielding ear of wheat, your arm, your knees,
the singing outlines through your skyblue dress
and—your eyes—velvet joy,—
I forget where I am. I become a springtime stream,
singing my heart out through every atom
of my blood. And then, and then—and only this is real—
we twine our hands together and we both
are equal in our dance.

And suddenly we go a stormy journey
through big dark woods, over night and day,
over time. The world hides somewhere in a corner.
I don't know who I am. I think: I'm evening gold, I'm you,
I'm even a swallow. . . . Shouts fly by, rivers, cities,
everything—in our dance, with red and violet
and green. You cry. I listen. Your look falls on me
like fire.
I think, you're a sailboat somewhere on the sea
and I a salty wind, in a duel with you.
You struggle. I spank you with foam. And we both
are equal in our dance.

1936

די ראַנדן פֿון אַ טײַך

איך זע פֿון הויכן באַרג, ווי ס׳בלאַנקען
די ראַנדן פֿון אַ טײַך. ביז העט
בײַם האָריזאָנט פֿאַרטונקלען זיי און צאַנקען
און לײַכטן זילבערגרין און פֿיאָלעט
אויף ס׳נײַ – און טונקלען ווידער. כ׳קוק אַרונטער
אין טײַך, וואָס לעשט מײַן פּנימס צונטער
און לײַטערט מיר מײַן גוף, מאַכט קלאָר אים,
און זאָג צו מיזרח, מערבֿ, צפֿון, דרום:

– פֿאַרנעמט און זעט,
ווי אונטן, צווישן בלעטערוואַרג און שטיבער,
איז אָנגעשריבן מיט אַ קאַלטער טײַכנשריפֿט מײַן נאָמען.

דערציילט פֿון אים דער גאָרער וועלט דעריבער.
אָמן.

The Banks of a River

From a high mountain I see how the banks of a river
shimmer. In the distance
near the horizon they darken and wrangle,
then light up silvergreen and violet,
then darken again. I look down
into the river where my face's tinder is quenched
and my body shines clear, transparent,
and I say to the east, west, north, south:

Look and see
how beneath choked leaves and houses
in cold riverwriting my name is written.

Broadcast it all over the world.
Amen.

1938

לאַנדשאַפֿט

דער הימל – ווי דער חלום פֿון אַ דולן,
ניטאָ אין אים די זון. זי בליט און קוועלט
מגולגל אין אַ הייסן, פֿולן
און ווילדן רויזנביימל אויפֿן פֿעלד.
דער ווינט איז אַ מכשף. ער פֿאַרקנעפּלט
דעם טאָג מיט נאַכט.
אַ וואָרצל צו אַ וואָרצל עפּעס פּרעפּלט.
אַ וואָלקן לאַכט
פֿון שלאָף. עס ווינקט פֿון וואַלד אַ בליציק אייגל.
ווי פֿאַלנדיקע שטערן פֿליִען פֿייגל.

Landscape

The sky—like a lunatic's dream—
has no sun in it. It blooms and laughs in a
hot full wild
rosetree in the meadow.
The wind is a magician. It buttons
        day to night.
A root babbles something to a root.
        A cloud laughs
        in its sleep. A lightning eye blinks from the wood.
        Birds fly by like falling stars.

1938

לידער צו אַ לונאַטיקערין

א

איך קען דיך פֿון לאַנג שוין, פֿון זינט
ביסט געווען אַן אַמפֿיביע.
געדענק נאָך די ערשטקייט פֿון זינד:
האָסט מיך ליב? – איך האָב ליב, יע.

מיר האָבן זיך ביידע געפּאָרט
אונטער זילבערנע שלאַקסן.
און אונדזער פֿאַרליבטשאַפֿט איז דאָרט
ווי אויף הייוון געוואַקסן.

ב

מיט אַ זילבערנעם בעזעם
קערסטו אויס פֿון מײַן חלום די שטויבן.
ווערט דאָס צימערל ריין. דורך די שויבן
גריסט אַ צווײַגעלע בעז איס.

און דײַן האַנט, וואָס דו שטרעקסט מיך צו זאַלבן,
פּרעסט די קנייטשעלעך אויס אויף מײַן שטערן,
ווי דײַן נאַכטהעמד אין פֿאַלבן
וואָס פֿאַרקנעפּלט דײַן ברוסט אויף אַ שטערן.

ג

איך וויל בלויז באַרירן דײַן סוד ווי אַ זעגל,
געבויגן פֿון שטורעם, באַרירט דאָס געאינד –
אַ סוד, וואָס צו איס איז פֿאַרזיגלט דאָס שטעגל
מיט טריוואַקס פֿון זינד.

אַהין איז מײַן גלוסט. איך מוז געבן אַן עפֿן
דערזען דעם פּייסאַזש וואָס דערשרעקט און באַרוט.
דײַן סוד, ווי דער טאָגגײַסט אין פֿידלשע עפֿן
מוז ווערן באַפֿאַכט פֿון מײַן פֿליגלדיק בלוט.

Songs to a Lady Moonwalker

1

I've known you since the time
  you were amphibian.
I remember our sin's firstness.
  you love me?—I love you, yes.

We paired ourselves together
  under silver weather.
Our love increased
  as though it rose from yeast.

2

With a silver broom
you sweep the dust from my dreams,
cleaning the little room. Through the pane
a twig of lilac gleams.

You stretch your hand to salve
and smooth my forehead clear
as your nightgown flutters in folds
and buttons your breast to a star.

3

Stormbent I'll brush your secret
as a sail brushes to a wave—
but your secret is tight with guilt,
the sealing wax of love.

My lust is: I must unveil
that landscape of terror and good.
Your secret that sings like a fiddle
must yield to my winging blood.

ד

ווער איז ער, דער דריטער, וואָס באַלד,
ווי כ׳צערטל דיך מאַכט ער אַ גוואַלד?
ס׳איז דאָך ער – דײַן געליבטער לעוואָניק,
וואָס רעגירט אויף אַ זילבערן טראָניק
אויף טונקלסטן צווײַגל פֿון וואַלד.

מיר קענען ניט זײַן זאַלבע דריט
ווען קוועקזילבער קילט דאָס געבליט.
ס׳גיט מײַן לײַב זיך פֿון קינאה אַ צאַפּל
ווען לעוואָניק זופּט אויס דײַן שוואַרצאַפּל
און באַקושט דיר מיט פּערל די טריט.

קלײַב איינעם פֿון ביידן אויס, קלײַב.
דעם צווייטן שלימזל פֿאַרטרײַב.
אָדער מאַך פֿון אַ מילב אים נאָך מילבער,
און פֿאַרברען אים אין שײַטער פֿון זילבער,
דו פֿויגל, דו חלום, דו ווײַב!

4

Who is he, that third one, as soon
as I fondle you, dares to protest?
It's your crazy love in the moon
who rules from a silver throne
on the blackest twig in the forest.

There can't be three of us
when quicksilver fills us with chills.
My envious skin will ripple
when that moonnik sucks out your pupil
and kisses your footsteps with pearls.

Choose, for choose you must.
Get rid of that bane of my life.
Nothing him less than dust,
let him burn in a silver log,
you bird, you dream, you wife.

ווי אַזוי?

ווי אַזוי און מיט וואָס וועסטו פֿילן
דײַן בעכער אין טאָג פֿון באַפֿרײַונג?
ביסטו גרייט אין דײַן פֿרייד צו דערפֿילן
דײַן פֿאַרגאַנגענהייטס פֿינצטערע שרײַונג
ווו עס גליווערן שאַרבנס פֿון טעג
אין אַ תּהום אָן אַ גרונט, אָן אַ דעק?

דו וועסט זוכן אַ שליסל צו פּאַסן
פֿאַר דײַנע פֿאַרהאַקטע שלעסער.
ווי ברויט וועסטו בײַסן די גאַסן
און טראַכטן: דער פֿריִער איז בעסער.
און די צײַט וועט דיך עקבערן שטיל
ווי אין פֿויסט אַ געפֿאַנגענע גריל.

און ס'וועט זײַן דײַן זכּרון געגליכן
צו אַן אַלטער פֿאַרשאָטענער שטאָט.
און דײַן דרויסיקער בליק וועט דאָרט קריכן
ווי אַ קראָט, ווי אַ קראָט ------

How

How and with what will you fill
your cup on the day of freedom?
In your joy are you willing to feel
yesterday's dark screaming,
where skulls of days congeal
in a pit with no bottom, no floor?

You will look for a key to fit
the lock shivered in the door.
You will bite the streets like bread
and think: it was better before.
And time will gnaw you mute
like a grasshopper caught in a fist.

They'll compare your memory
to an ancient buried town.
And your alien eyes will tunnel down
like a mole, like a mole . . .

Vilna Ghetto, February 14, 1943

לויבליד פֿאַר אַן אָקס

קומט באַוווּנדערן מײַן אָקס.
ניטאָ צו אים קיין גלײַכן.
זײַן טאַטע איז געווען די זון,
זײַן מאַמע – די לבֿנה.

ווײַסער פֿון די שפּריצן מילך די ערשטע
בײַ אַ פֿרוי,
ווען די גיט צו זייגן, איז די ווײַסקייט פֿון זײַן שטערן.

אין זײַנע אויגן קאָן מען זען די צוקונפֿט.
נאָר איר זאָלט
בעסער זיי ניט עפֿענען
אין רגעס ווען זיי דרימלען.

די הערנער זענען מאַסטן פֿון אַ שיף,
אַזאַ וואָס פֿירט אין בויך אַפֿולע אוצרות.

מיידלעך ווערן אַנדערש אינעם שימער פֿון זײַן פּראַכט.
אין זייער בלוט –
אַ וואַרעמקייט פֿון אומבאַקאַנטע מײַלער.

קומט באַוווּנדערן מײַן אָקס.
ניטאָ צו אים קיין גלײַכן.

ווו ער באָדט זיך – ווערן זיס די טײַכן.

Song of Praise for an Ox
(from the African Cycle)

Come marvel at my ox.
He has no equal.
His father was the sun,
his mother—the moon.

Whiter than the first spurts of milk
from a woman
giving suck, so is the whiteness of his brow.

In his eyes you can see the future,
but don't pry
them open
if they're drowsy at the moment.

His horns are the masts of a ship
carrying great treasure in its belly.

Girls are transformed in the shimmer of his splendor.
They feel in their blood
the warmth of unknown mouths.

Come marvel at my ox.
He has no equal.

Whatever he bathes—the rivers become sweet.

1950

פּאָעזיע

אַ טונקל פֿיאָלעטע פֿלוים
די לעצטע אויפֿן בוים
דין־הײַטלעך און צאַרט ווי אַ שוואַרצאַפּל,
וואָס האָט בײַ נאַכט אין טוי געלאָשן
ליבע, זעונג, צאַפּל,
און מיטן מאָרגן־שטערן אין דער טוי
געוואָרן גרינגער –
דאָס איז פּאָעזיע. ריר זי אָן אַזוי
מען זאָל ניט זען קיין סימן פֿון די פֿינגער.

Poetry

The last dark violet
plum on the tree,
delicate and tender as the pupil of an eye,
blots out in the dewy night
all love, visions, trembling,
and at the morningstar the dew
becomes airier—
that's poetry. Touch it without
letting it show the print of your fingers.

1954

אונטער דער ערד

צוויטשערן פֿייגל דען אונטער דער ערד
מיט געטלעכע טרערן
פֿאַרשטיקטע אין העלדזעלעך דינע,
אָדער דאָס פֿלאַטערן אונטער דער ערד
איינמאָליקע ווערטער, ווי ניט קיין געזעענע פֿייגל?

ווױהין מײַנע פֿיס האָבן שׂכל צו שפּאַנען,
איבער שניי, איבער היי, איבער שיכּורן פֿײַער,
פֿילן זיי ווערטער,
נשמות פֿון ווערטער,
אַ שאָד וואָס די פֿיס מײַנע קאָנען ניט האַלטן קיין בלײַער . . .

ווי אַ שלאַנגען־באַשווערער
פֿאַרהאַלט איך די פֿיס אינעם גאַנג:
דאָ און דאָ און דאָ.
דאָ זענען זיי דאָ.
איינמאָליקע שטילקייט.
איינמאָליקע ערטער.
און איך גראָב מיט די הענט – מײַנע בייניקע רידלען,
ביז וואַנען עס פּלאַצן
די שוואַרצע פּאַלאַצן
ווּ ס'פֿלאַטערן ווערטער
באַהאַלטן אין פֿידלען.

Under the Earth

Are there birds twittering under the earth,
choking back
their holy tears in their thin necks,
or is that throbbing under the earth
once-used words that seem invisible birds?

Wherever my feet have the wisdom to walk,
over snow, over hay, over drunken fire,
they feel words,
the souls of words,
it's a pity my feet can't hold a pencil . . .

Like a snakecharmer
I stop my feet in their going:
here and here and here
here they are, here.
Once-used silence.
Once-used places.
And I dig with my hands—bony spades,
down to where the black
palaces burst,
where words throb
hidden in violins.

1956

די פֿידלרויז

פֿון תּחית־המתים־דיק וואַרעמען רעגן
פֿאַוואָלינקע נעמט זיך צעבליִען, באַוועגן
(בײַנאַנד מיט דער קינדהייט אין אַלטן זכּרון)
די פֿידלרויז אינעם שוואַרצערדיקן אָרון.

די פֿידלרויז דאַרף שוין אַצינד ניט קיין פֿידלער,
ניטאָ מער קיין לויבער, ניטאָ מער קיין זידלער.
זי שפּילט אָן אַ שפּילער מיט פֿרייד און אמונה
לכּבֿוד אַ ווידערגעבוירענער סטרונע.

לכּבֿוד אַ סטרונע, לכּבֿוד איר ציטער,
לכּבֿוד אַ בין וואָס איר האָניק איז ביטער
נאָר זיס איז איר שטאָך, אַזוי זאַפֿטיק און קווייטיק –
לכּבֿוד אַ ווידערגעבוירענעם ווייטיק.

The Fiddle Rose

From resurrecting warm rain
she begins slowly to blossom, to grow—
(together with the childhood of my aged memory)—
the fiddle rose in her earth-black coffin.

The fiddle rose doesn't need a fiddler,
there's no one left to praise or curse her.
She plays without a player, with joy and faith
in honor of a reborn string.

In honor of a string, in honor of its vibration,
in honor of a bee whose honey is bitter
but whose sting is sweet, so juicy and flowerlike—
in honor of a reborn pain.

פֿינגערשפּיצן

. . . און איין מאָל אין אַ ווינטערנאַכט,
ווען כ'האָב די קאַלטע פֿינגער
אַרײַנגעטאָן אין קעשענע פֿון פּעלצל,
דערפֿילט האָבן די פֿינגערשפּיצן לעבעדיקן זײַד –
אַ צאַרטינקע גן־עדן־טויב
אין טויבנשלאַק פֿון קעשענע.

געווען איז עס ניט מער ווי אַ פּאַפּירל, וואָס כ'האָב פֿריִער
אין בוידעמשטיבל
אָנגעקאָרמעט צערטלעך
מיט וואָרקענדיקע ווערטער.
און ווײַל מיר איז געווען אַ שאָד מיט דעם זיך צו צעשיידן,
און אויך דערפֿאַר ווײַל כ'האָב עס ניט געטרויט מײַן רויטער קאַץ,
ס'פּאַפּירל האָב איך מיטגענומען אויף אַ פֿרייד־באַגעגעניש
אין דרויסן, וווּ עס פּלאַצן שוואַרצע שפּיגלען פֿון די שאָטנס.

נאָר מײַנע פֿינגערשפּיצן זענען דעמאָלט
געוואָרן שיכּור פֿון דער צאַרטקייט. אַנדערש ניט: געפֿאַנגען
אין קעשענע בײַ מיר
איז די נשמה פֿון דער וועלט.

און מײַנע פֿינגערשפּיצן קאָנען שווערן:
אַזאַ מין צאַרטקייט האָבן זיי אין ערגעץ ניט געפֿילט.

Fingertips

. . . Once on a winter night,
when I put my cold fingers
into the pocket of my fur jacket,
my fingertips felt living silk—
a tender dove of paradise
in the dovecote of my pocket.

It was only a fragment of paper that I had once
gently fed
in my garret
with cooing words.
And because I felt it was a shame to part with them
and also because I didn't trust my red cat with it,
I took the paper with me to a joyous rendezvous
outside, where black mirrors cracked in the shadows.

Then my fingertips became
drunk with tenderness. Why not? Trapped
in my pocket
was the soul of the world.

And my fingertips can swear
they have never felt such tenderness anywhere,

אַפֿילו נאָכן אָפּדעקן אַ פֿרילינגדיקן וואָלקנדל
פֿון האַרץ פֿון דער געליבטער.

נאָר הײַנט, ווען כ׳האָב פֿאַרלוירן, צי ס׳האָט ווער אַרויסגעגנבֿעט,
פֿון קעשענע מײַן וועלט –
זיי זענען ווידער
געוואָרן שיכּור פֿון אַ צאַרטקייט,
מײַנע פֿינגערשפּיצן.

די צאַרטקייט פֿונעם יונגן מאָצאַרט, פֿון אַ סטראַדיוואַריוס?
די צאַרטקייט פֿון אַ רויז, באַשיצט מיט אײַפֿערזוכט פֿון דאָרן?

זיי האָבן אין דער קעשענע באַרירט הײַנט מײַן זכּרון.

even after undressing a little spring cloud
in the heart of my beloved.

Just today, when either I had lost it or someone had stolen
the world from my pocket—
they became drunk
from the tenderness again—
my fingertips.

The tenderness of young Mozart, of a Stradivarius?
The tenderness of a rose, protected by the jealousy of thorns?

In my pocket today they brushed against my memory.

1971

טעלע מײַן שוועסטער

טעלע מײַן שוועסטער האָט צו דרײַצן יאָר געקענט
אויסנווייניק האַלב סלאָוואַצקי. ס׳האָבן אַזש די ווענט
פֿונעם בוידעמשטיבל, די צונויפֿגעלאָטעט־בלאָע,
מיטן טויבנשלאָק דערבײַ, געשמייכלט פֿון הנאה,
ווען זי האָט פֿון איר זכּרון ווי אַן אָפֿן בוך
דעקלאַמירט פֿאַר שאָטנס אין אַ ווינקל זײַן „קרול דוך".

צו דערגיין דעם סוד פֿון איר זכּרון און פֿאַנטאַזיע
פֿלעגן אירע נײַגעריקע לערער פֿון גימנאַזיע
קומען צו דער מאַמען, זי מוז וויסן דאָך אַוודאי:
ווען אַ שטייגער האָט באַוויזן אויסצולערנען טעלע
אויסנווייניק לעבעדיקע שטיקער פֿון איליאַדע?
וואָסער קאָמפּעטענטש רעדט זי אײַן צו דענקען שאָפּענהויעריש?
אָדער גאָר: פֿון וואַנען וויס זי וועגן מעטאַפֿיזיק?
וווּנדער איז געווען איר וויסן. ריזיק.
ס׳האָבן זיך געפֿילט אַנטקעגן טעלען די לערער
נידעריק און פּויעריש.

טעלע מײַן שוועסטער האָט אַ מאָל פֿאַר נאַכט (אין דרויסן
האָט אַ זיסער פֿראָסט געזאָדן ווי בײַם לעשן קאַלך)
אָנגעטאָן די וואָליקלעך, דאָס וויאָלעטע מאַנטעלע
מיטן רויטן אונטערשלאָק, און איז אַוועק שפּאַצירן.
איינינקע אַליין אין פֿעלד שפּאַצירן.

My Sister Ethel

My sister Ethel at thirteen knew
by heart half of Slowacki. The very walls
of our attic home, patched-together blue
with pigeon cotes nearby, smiled with pleasure
when she recited Slowacki's "King Spirit" from memory
as though from an open book, for the shadows in the corner.

Her curious teachers from the high school
used to come to her mother to discover
the secret of her memory, her imagination: did she know
when, for example, Ethel had learned by heart
those living passages from the Iliad?
What intellectual told her to think like Schopenhauer?
Or simply: where did she learn about metaphysics?
Her knowledge was a miracle. Immense.
In front of Ethel the teacher felt
inferior, like a peasant.

One day before nightfall my sister Ethel (outside
a sweet frost sizzled like quicklime)
put on her felt boots, her purple coat
with the red lining, and went out to walk.
To walk all alone in the fields.

עטעלע האָט ליב געהאַט פֿאַרגאַנגענע קאָלירן.
וואָסער מין פֿאַרנאַכט איז דאָס געווען, עס האָט אין איר
אָנגעצונדן זיך אַ חלום פונקט אַזאַ קאָליר.
לענגער דאָרט געבליבן הענגען ווי די האַלבע זון
צווישן פֿײַערציין פֿון וואָלקן. אפֿשר האָט מײַן שוועסטער
מיטנעמען געוואָלט אַ שטיקל זון, די זון־ירושה?

עטעלע מײַן שוועסטער האָט פֿון דעמאָלט אָן געברענט.
פֿונעם בוידעמשטיבל האָט בײַ נאַכט אַרויסגעלויכטן
יענער זונפֿאַרגאַנג, נאָר זי האָט לענגער
אויפֿהאַלטן אים ניט געקענט אין מוח.

אויסגעלאָשן האָט ער זיך מיט עטעלען צוזאַמען
אינעם בוידעמשטיבל מיט די גליטשיק הויכע טרעפ.

ס׳זענען בלויז געבליבן אירע שוואַרצע לאַנגע צעפ
צווישן די פֿאַרגרייטע ווײַסע בגדים פֿון דער מאַמען.

צוואַנציק יאָר האָט עטעלען באַקלאָגט די מאַמע, צוואַנציק יאָר,
ווײַס געוואָרן זענען אין די טויטע צעפ די האָר,
ביז בערלין האָט זיך דערבאַרעמט, ניט געקאָנט מער זען און הערן,
אָנגעלאָפֿן – און דערשאָסן באַלד מײַן מאַמעס טרערן.

Ethel loved the colors of sunset.
Whatever kind of twilight it was, it ignited
a dream in her exactly the same color.
Stayed hanging there longer than the half-sun
between the fireteeth of a cloud. Perhaps my sister
wanted to take a bit of sun with her, as her inheritance?

From then on, my sister Ethel burned.
From our attic home at night that sunset
shone, but she could no longer
hold it in her brain.

It burned out together with Ethel
in the attic home with the slippery high steps.

Only her long black braids remained
among the white garments her mother prepared for her.

For twenty years her mother mourned for Ethel, twenty years:
the dead braid of hair became white,
until Berlin took pity on her, could no longer see or hear,
attacked—and quickly shot my mother's tears.

1972

תּפֿילה פֿאַר אַ קראַנקן חבֿר

רשעים האָבן צו פֿיל כּוח,
געוווּנג פֿאַר זיי די קראַפֿט פֿון האָזן.
איז קאַרמע אַן מיט גנאָד אַ שוואַכן,
אַט ליגט ער דאָך: האַלב מענטש האַלב לײַלעך.

זײַן תּפֿילה בין איך. זײַנע ליפּן
פֿאַרלוירן האָבן שוין די ווערטער.
זיי זענען אויסגעריבטע מושלען
אָן ווידערקול, אָן זאַלץ, אָן פּערל.

ער דאַרף נאָך אָנצינדן אַ שורה
אין היכל פֿון זײַן טונקעלער קאָנורע.
ער דאַרף די יונגע קיניגין פֿון בינען
באַגלייטן צו דעם בין־שטערן באַגינען.

איך האָב געזען אַ פֿיש דערלאַנגען
אַ שפּרונג פֿון ים־האַרץ ביזן וואָלקן
און מיטשלעפּן מיט זיך דעם וואָלקן —
איז ווינציקער פֿון פֿיש מײַן חבֿר?

אַנשטאָט די קײַקעלעך די רויטע
אין זײַנע אָדערן גאָר שווימען
רויט־פֿידעלעך פֿון דיר געמײַסטערט,
קיין צווייטער וועט אויף זיי ניט שפּילן.

ער דאַרף נאָך הערן ווי זײַן דפֿק
איז פֿרילינג־רעגן אין זײַן לײַב און לויפֿיק.
ער דאַרף נאָר זופּן חלום, שעפּן גלויבן,
און שפּעטן האַרבסט — פֿאַרקיטעווען די שויבן.

Prayer for a Sick Friend

The wicked have too much power,
it would be enough for them to have the strength of rabbits.
Feed the weak one with mercy,
for here he lies: half man, half bedsheet.

I'm his prayer. His lips
have already lost the words.
They're despoiled seashells
without echo, without salt, without pearls.

He still needs to light up a sentence
in the temple of his dark burrow.
He must accompany the young
queen of the bees to her be-starred dawn.

I've seen a fish leap
from the sea-heart to the clouds
and carry the clouds with him—
Is my friend less than a fish?

Instead of little red circles
in his veins, red fiddles
are swimming, mastered by you—
no one else can play them.

He must still hear how his pulse
is spring-rain running in his body.
He must still sip dreams, keep faith,
and—in late fall—putty the windows.

1972

חלום וועגן אַן אַלטן הומאָריסט

לעצטע נאַכט האָב איך געהאַט אַ חלום,
איז נאָכגעגאַנגען מיר זײַן פּאַראַדאָקס
ביז טיף אין טאָג אַרײַן: עס איז אַ פֿרוי געגאַנגען
שפּאַצירן מיט אַן אָקס.

דער אָקס – האָב איך געוווּסט – איז מײַנער אַ באַקאַנטער,
אַ ייִד אַ הומאָריסט. ער איז אויף צרות,
אַן עובֿר־בטל, טויב און בלינדעוואַטע,
מיט אַ פּנים פֿון אַן אַלטן סריס.
פֿון זײַנע וויצן לאַכט מען נישט. ער שמעקט מיט קבֿר.

איצט איז ער, דער אָקס דער גרויסער, רויטער, פֿעטער,
געגאַנגען שטאָלץ – און ס'האָט די פֿרוי באַגלייט אים
מיט אַ מינע אַ קאָקעטער,
ביז ער האָט געלאָזט זי הינטער זיך
און האָט מיט גבֿורה
אָוועקגעשפּאַנט אַנטקעגן עפּעס
אַ שור־המועדיקער אַוואַנטורע.
פֿריילעך און פֿרעך האָט ער געשפּאַנט,
נאָר איך האָב גוט געוווּסט, אַז דאָס איז ער –
דער אויסגעדינטער הומאָריסט, דער עקס־טאַלאַנט,
וואָס איז אַלט און אומעטיק־צעקנוידערט,
און פֿון דעם נײַעם וויץ זײַנעם האָט מיר אין שלאָף
געשווידערט.

AARON ZEITLIN

A Dream About an Aged Humorist

Last night I had a dream
whose paradox followed me
late into the day: a woman was
walking with an ox.

The ox—as I knew—is an acquaintance of mine,
a Jew, a humorist. He's in trouble,
senile, deaf, and half-blind,
with the face of an old eunuch.
They don't laugh at his jokes. He smells of the grave.

Now he, that big ox, red, fat,
was walking proudly—and the woman with him
had the look of a flirt,
until he left her behind
and violently
rushed off to meet some kind of
bullish adventure.
He strutted about joyful and fresh
but I knew perfectly well it was he—
the worndown humorist, the ex-talent,
old and sadly wrinkled all over,
and when I thought of his new joke in my sleep,
I shuddered.

אַ ליידיקע דירה

ס'האָט מיך געצויגן זען אַ דירה,
ווּ כ'האָב אַ מאָל געוווינט.
זי איז געשטאַנען ליידיק
און ס'האָט זיך איר געחלומט אַ פּאַרשוין,
וואָס האָט אַ מאָל דאָרט געפּאַרשוינט —
איך.

שורות,
וואָס כ'האָב דאָרט געשריבן.
האָבן זיך געקליבן
אַרום די פֿענצטער
קופּעסוויַיז, ווי פֿייגל פֿאַרן אָפּפֿלי.

ס'איז געקראָכן
און שטיל געזאָטן
אַן אַסטראַל־גוף פֿון אַן אינזעקט,
וואָס כ'האָב אַ מאָל צעטראָטן.

קוימקוימיקייטן פֿלערליי
האָבן געשטעקט
אין די ווינקלען, אין שאָטן,
ווי שטויב אונטער אַ באַרשט,
מיט מיַיזישער שרעק
געזוכט אַ שפּאַלט צום אַנטרינען.

אַ שרעטל,
וואָס איז געלעגן נאַקעט ביַי אַ וואַנט,
איז אויף מיר אַרויפֿגעשפּרונגען:
טאַטע, וואָס מאַכסטו?

The Empty Apartment

I was drawn to look at an apartment
where I once lived.
It stood empty,
dreaming of a person
who once personned there—
me.

Lines
I wrote there
gathered themselves
around the windows
in flocks, like birds before flight.

Crawling
and quietly seething
was the astral body of an insect
I once squashed.

All kinds of almost nothings
were stuck
in the corners, in the shadows,
like dust under a brush,
looking with mousey fright
for a crack to escape into.

A very small imp
who lay naked under a wall,
jumped up at me:
Papa, how are you?

אין מיטן צימער איז געשטאַנען אַ מחשבֿה.
זי איז געשטאַנען אַ פֿאַרלוירענע, געטראַכט
פֿון יענעם, וואָס האָט אַ מאָל זי געטראַכט
אָט־דאָ אין אַ פֿאַרנאַכט:
פֿון מיר.

אַז זי האָט מיך דערזען,
האָט זי זיך אַ ריס געטאָן פֿון אָרט
און מיך גענומען זידלען.
דו ביסט, — האָט זי געזאָגט, — אַ פֿינצטערער פֿאַררעטער,
אַן אַנטלויפֿער, אַ פֿאַרשווינדער,
אַ געבוירער,
וואָס לאָזט אויף הפֿקר זײַנע קינדער.

In the middle of the room stood a thought.
She stood there lost in thought
about the one who once thought about her
here one evening:
about me.

And when she noticed me,
she tore herself from the spot
and began to revile me.
You are, she said, a dark betrayer,
a runner-away, a disappearer,
a begetter
who abandons his offspring.

טעקסט

מיר אַלע –
שטיינער, מענטשן, שערבלעך גלאָז אין זון,
קאָנסערוון־פּושקעס, קעץ און ביימער –
זענען אילוסטראַציעס צו אַ טעקסט.

ערגעץ ווו דאַרף מען אונדז נישט האָבן.
דאָרט לייענט מען דעם טעקסט אַליין –
די בילדער פֿאַלן אָפּ ווי טויטע גלידער.

ווען טויטווינט גיט אַ בלאָז אין טיפֿן גראָז
און רוימט אַראָפּ פֿון מערבֿ אַלע בילדער,
וואָס וואָלקנס האָבן אויפֿגעשטעלט –
קומט נאַכט און לייענט שטערן.

Text

We all—
stones, people, little shards of glass in the sun,
tin cans, cats and trees—
are illustrations to a text.

In some places they don't need us.
In some places they only read the text—
the pictures fall off like shriveled parts.

When a death-wind blows in the deep grass
and clears off from the west all the pictures
that the clouds set up—then
night comes and reads the stars.

TEXTS USED

Celia Dropkin: *In a Hot Wind*, New York, 1959.

Jacob Glatstein: *From All My Work*, New York, 1956; *The Joy of the Yiddish Word*, New York, 1961; *A Jew from Lublin*, 1966; *Songs from Right to Left*, 1971.

M. L. Halpern: *In New York*, New York, 1919; 1934.

Rachel Korn: *Home and Homelessness*, Buenos Aires, 1948; *Kismet*, Buenos Aires, 1957; *The Other Side of the Poem*, 1962.

Moyshe Kulbak: *Poems and Songs*, Vilna, 1929; *Selected Works*, New York, 1953.

Zisha Landau: *Poems*, New York, 1937.

H. Leivick: *Songs to Eternity*, New York, 1959; *Collected Works*, Buenos Aires, 1963.

Itzik Manger: Songs and Ballads, New York, 1952.

Anna Margolin: *Poems*, New York, 1929.

Kadya Molodowsky: *November Nights*, Vilna, 1927; *Only King David Remained*, New York, 1946; *Light from a Thorntree*, Buenos Aires, 1965.

Leyb Naydus: *Lyrics*, Warsaw, 1926.

Melech Ravitch: *Lyric, Satiric, National, Social and Philosophical Poems*, Buenos Aires, 1946; *Poems from My Poems*, Montreal, 1954.

Abraham Sutzkever: *Collected Works (I and II)*, Tel Aviv, 1963; *The Fiddle Rose: Poems 1970–1972*, Detroit, 1990.

Aaron Zeitlin: *Collected Poems (I and II)*, New York, 1957.

NOTES ON THE POETS

CELIA DROPKIN, born in Russia in 1888, came to New York in 1912 and became a member of the Insichists. She was a painter and wrote stories as well as poetry. She was beautiful, passionate, defiant, and unruly. She died in New York in 1956.

JACOB GLATSTEIN was born in Lublin in 1896. When he came to the United States in 1914 he was already a poet, although he didn't begin to write in Yiddish until 1919. One of the founders of the Insichists, he was also an outstanding journalist, novelist, and critic. He died in 1971.

MOYSHE LEYB HALPERN was born in East Galicia in 1886. At the age of twelve he went to Vienna, where he wrote his first poetry in German. In 1908 he came to the United States to escape military service. He was a member of Di Yunge group of Yiddish poets in New York, as well as a journalist and artist. He died in New York in 1933.

RACHEL KORN was born in Galicia in 1898. Her first literary efforts were written in Polish. It was not until 1919 that she began to write and publish in Yiddish. When the Nazis invaded Poland, she escaped to Sweden and then to Russia. After the Liberation by the Allies she lived in Montreal and Florida. She died in Montreal in 1982.

MOYSHE KULBAK, born in Smorgon in 1896 of peasant parents, first wrote poems in Hebrew. He went to Germany with a troupe of Vilna performers, then returned to teach Yiddish literature in a high school in Vilna. In 1928 he went to Soviet Russia where he wrote plays for the Yiddish State Theater. He was warned by the Moscow police for writing a controversial play, was arrested, and disappeared mysteriously in 1937. He was reported to have died in 1940.

ZISHA LANDAU, born in Poland in 1889, arrived in the United States in 1906. He translated Russian and German poetry into Yiddish, and was particularly fond of Heine, to whom his Hebrew teacher had introduced him. An early member of Di Yunge, he died in New York in 1937.

H. LEIVICK, whose real name was Leivick Halpern, was born in Russia in 1888. He was arrested for political activity and sent to Siberia in 1912. Through the intervention of friends in the United States, he escaped to New York in 1913. He wrote many plays and is especially know for his great verse drama, The Golem. He died in New York in 1962.

ITZIK MANGER, born in Romania in 1901, spent his childhood in Germany. Greatly influenced by the German lyric poets, especially Rilke, and by old Yiddish ballads, may of his poems have come into the repertory of Yiddish folksongs. He lived in London after the Second World War, and came to New York in 1951. He died in Israel in 1969.

ANNA MARGOLIN was born in 1887 in Brest-Litovsk, Russia. She came to the United States, married the Hebrew novelist Moses Stavsky, and went to live in Palestine for a few years. A member of the Insichists, she was famous for her rowdy behavior in the lower East Side cafeteria where the poets met to discuss their work. She later became a recluse and died in 1952.

KADYA MOLODOWSKY was born in Lithuania in 1894. She wrote many poems, novels, short stories, and plays about Jewish life in Poland. She is know particularly for her children's poetry and stories. In Warsaw, where she taught school and published poetry, she was persecuted by the Fascist police for her socialist activities. She came to New York in 1935, where she continued to write and publish. She died in 1975.

LEYB NAYDUS was born in 1890 in Grodne, Polish Lithuania, of a well-to-do father who wrote poetry in Hebrew. He went to school in Bialystok, where he was thrown out for socialist activities, then attended a Vilna gymnasium. He wrote his first poetry in Russian, then turned to Yiddish in 1907. He contributed to Yiddish literary magazines and wrote translations of Russian and French poetry. He died in Vilna in 1918.

MELECH RAVITCH, whose real name is Zachariah Berger, was born in 1893 in Eastern Galicia. He traveled extensively, lived for a while in Australia, and then went to live in Montreal, Canada, where he died in 1976.

ABRAHAM SUTZKEVER, born in 1913 in Smorgon, escaped with his family to Siberia when Smorgon was burned by the Cossacks. In 1922 he came to Vilna and joined the Young Vilna group of poets. He fought in the Vilna Ghetto in the Second World War, saved the archives from the Jewish Museum, of which he was curator, escaped to the woods, where he fought with the Partisans, and later joined the Russian army. He settled in Israel after the Liberation, where he now publishes a prestigious Yiddish literary journal, *Di Goldene Keyt*.

AARON ZEITLIN, born in 1889 in Uwaroviche, White Russia, moved to Warsaw in 1907. He visited Palestine and the United States in 1920, then settled in New York before the Second World War. His father, a writer and scholar, was killed in the Warsaw Ghetto. He published poetry and articles in both Yiddish and Hebrew. He died in New York in 1973.